FORGIVENESS

FORGIVENESS
God's Gift of Love

Lucy Fuchs, Ph.D.

ALBA · HOUSE   NEW · YORK

SOCIETY OF ST. PAUL, 2187 VICTORY BLVD., STATEN ISLAND, NEW YORK 10314

Library of Congress Cataloging-in-Publication Data

Fuchs, Lucy.
    Forgiveness: God's gift of love / Lucy Fuchs.
        p.   cm.
    Includes bibliographical references.
    ISBN 0-8189-0571-9
    1. Forgiveness — Religious aspects — Christianity. 2. Christian
life — Catholic authors.   I. Title.
    BV4647.F55F82   1990   89-48955
    241'.4 — dc20   CIP

Designed, printed and bound in the United States of
America by the Fathers and Brothers of the
Society of St. Paul, 2187 Victory Boulevard,
Staten Island, New York 10314, as part of their
communications apostolate.

Printing Information:

Current Printing - first digit   2 3 4 5 6 7 8 9 10 11 12

Year of Current Printing - first year shown
1990   1991   1992   1993   1994   1995   1996   1997

To

BETTY DeANGELIS

and all the loving caring people
of Nativity Parish in Brandon, Florida

Acknowledgments

This book has taken many years to write, although the actual writing extended only over a few months. The idea of forgiveness is something most of us, including me, learned as children. As time went on, our knowledge was increased and refined through many others with whom we came in contact. Not only did we learn about forgiveness, but we experienced it many times ourselves, both in giving and receiving. As I wrote this book, I had a rich reservoir of experience to draw on.

I acknowledge all the input others have had in the writing of this book, either directly or indirectly. First of all have been my parents, brothers, sisters, friends, and co-workers, as well as my teachers and students. I thank especially my colleagues in the Christopher Leadership Course who have been such good examples of enthusiastic and joyous living, and of always searching for the positive approach. But above all, I thank my husband, Frank, who, as ever, gave his full support and help on this book.

Material from *Healing Prayer* by Barbara Shlemon
Copyright © 1976 by Ave Maria Press, Notre Dame, IN 46556.
All rights reserved. Used with permission of the publisher.
Material from *Ten Christians* by Boniface Hanley
Copyright © 1979 by St. Anthony's Guild, Paterson, NJ 07509.
All rights reserved. Used with permission of the publisher, Ave Maria Press, Notre Dame, IN 46556.
Material from *Healing Life's Hurts* by Dennis & Matthew Linn
Copyright © 1978 by Paulist Press.

Table of Contents

I.

The Matter of Forgiveness

1.

Forgiveness

You have been hurt. The pain of the hurt arouses anger and you feel like lashing out at the other person. You think of things you could say to the person. Your temperature rises and your face grows red. You walk faster. You clench your fists. You want to strike the other person.

Time goes by. Every time you think of the hurt, you feel the pain again. Years may go by, but the wound is still there, now covered perhaps by a scab. This scab is very susceptible to further injury. If you bump it, bleeding is likely to start all over again. It may fester and cause infection if you do not allow it to heal.

The only way to heal such wounds is to forgive and to be forgiven. What does it mean to forgive? How can we forgive? How can we let go of the pain? Anyone who has suffered a real hurt from another person, anyone who has felt deep anger and even rage against that person, knows how very difficult forgiveness is.

As time goes by we find that we have received many hurts in our lives. Sadly we also find that we ourselves have hurt others and caused them pain. There is so much to forgive and so much forgiveness to ask for. We need to forgive our parents and other members of our families who love us but who may have hurt us. We need to forgive those who definitely do not love us, and those who hate everyone. We need to forgive ourselves too, and we need to forgive the situation of the world that we find ourselves in.

The only way to heal life's hurts is to extend our forgiveness to everyone possible and to ask forgiveness from them all, starting with God himself. Forgiveness not only heals us; it sets us free. Until this happens we do not even know how much we are under the sway of our anger and resentment. Forgiveness frees both us and the ones who have hurt us.

Forgiveness is at the very heart of the Christian message. Jesus said that he did not come to condemn but to save (Jn 3:17). It is not the well who need the physician but the sick (Mt 9:12), and he, the divine physician came to heal. The hope he held out to people was one of forgiveness. Some of the most touching stories in the Scriptures are of sinners who approached Jesus and were forgiven (cf. Jn 8:3ff), often without even saying a word on their part, certainly without lengthy incriminations on the part of Jesus. Christianity is not a religion of perfect people, but of forgiven people.

In spite of that, forgiveness is difficult. We seem to want to hold on to the hurts that others have given us. Our anger or even rage at others envelopes us and we find it hard to break out of it. On the other hand, when we have sinned or offended others, we feel guilt, and sometimes we seem to have as much trouble letting go of this guilt as we do of our anger. Perhaps this means that we are not ready to forgive ourselves, or to believe that others, including God, can really forgive us either.

Models of forgiveness can help us learn to forgive. When we see persons who have suffered greatly at the hands of others forgive, we find that we can learn to forgive too. The greatest example of all is, of course, Jesus, who forgave his executioners — and us — from the cross: "Father, forgive them for they know not what they do."

But we need help to forgive. This is not something that seems to come naturally to us. Our best help comes from Jesus who offers us his grace of forgiveness. We also need the help and support of other people, as well as their forgiveness. As we are forgiven, we can learn to forgive. As we forgive others, we can rest assured that we ourselves are forgiven (cf. Lk 6:37).

2.

What Do The Scriptures Say About Forgiveness?

a. The Old Testament

The entire Old Testament is the story of God's dealing with his people. He creates them, he loves them and cares for them. But they are always moving away from him, forgetting him, turning to idols. At times God is very angry with his people. Once he says he even repents that he ever created them. Sometimes he punishes them to bring them back. Sometimes he sends prophets to warn them. Always he appeals to his people. Eventually they repent and he forgives them. He always does.

As God forgives his people, he tells them again and again that they must forgive others.

The Old Testament gives us many beautiful examples of forgiveness. In Genesis we read the story of Jacob and Esau. Jacob had connived to win his brother's birthright and Esau was angry enough to kill his brother. His mother Rebecca urged Jacob to leave for his own safety. He did so, but years later he returned. On his way he saw Esau arriving with four hundred men. He was afraid for his life. Jacob feared also for his wives and children.

The story continues: (Genesis 33:3, 4) "He himself went ahead of them and bowed to the ground seven times before going up to his brother. But Esau ran to meet him, took him in his arms and held him close and wept."

At that moment Esau forgave all.

Later Jacob's son Joseph was sold into Egypt by his envious brothers. During a time of famine they went to Egypt to buy grain and were ushered in to meet with Joseph, now governor of the land, who recognized them immediately, although they did not recognize him. Here would be his chance for revenge. But Joseph acted differently. Genesis 45:3-8 tells us: "Joseph said to his brothers, 'I am Joseph. Is my father really still alive?' His brothers could not answer him, they were so dismayed at the sight of him. Then Joseph said to his brothers, 'Come closer to me.' When they had come closer to him he said, 'I am your brother Joseph whom you sold into Egypt. But now, do not grieve, do not reproach yourselves for having sold me here, since God sent me before you to preserve your lives. For this is the second year there has been famine in the country, and there are still five years to come of no plowing or reaping. God sent me before you to make sure that your race would have survivors in the land and to save your lives, many lives at that. So it was not you who sent me here but God, and he has made me father to Pharaoh, lord of all his household and administrator of the whole land of Egypt.'"

What a man of faith Joseph is, who is able not only to forgive but even to see the hand of God in the injustices that he endured.

But at the death of Jacob, Joseph's brothers were still

uncertain. They were afraid that now Joseph could have his sweet revenge (Genesis 50:18-21).

"His brothers came themselves and fell down before him. 'We present ourselves before you,' they said, 'as your slaves.' But Joseph answered them, 'Do not be afraid; is it for me to put myself in God's place? The evil you planned to do me has by God's design been turned to good, that he might bring about, as indeed he has, the deliverance of a numerous people. So you need not be afraid; I myself will provide for you and your dependents.' In this way he reassured them with words that touched their hearts."

This is a very touching story. Such loving forgiveness is so rare that we hardly believe it. We need to hear it more than once before we are reassured.

Moses, too, is an example of a forgiving person. In Numbers 12 we read of how Miriam and Aaron spoke against Moses (12:2-3): "They said, 'Has Yahweh spoken to Moses only? Has he not spoken to us too?' Yahweh heard this. Now Moses was the most humble of men, the humblest man on earth."

As a humble man, he did not take offense and when God punished them, particularly Miriam, Moses prayed for them. At his prayer, God forgave them.

David shows us an example of forgiveness. When Saul sent his armies after him, David once caught Saul alone and could have killed him. Instead he cut off the border of his cloak. Later he regretted having done even that. But he called after Saul (1 Samuel 24:9-11):

" 'My lord and king!' Saul looked behind him and David bowed to the ground and did homage. Then David said to Saul, 'Why do you listen to the men who say to you, "David means to harm you?" Why, your own eyes have seen today how Yahweh put you in my power in the cave and how I refused to kill you, but spared you.' "

Saul recognized this goodness (18-20): " 'You are a more upright man than I,' he said to David, 'for you have repaid me with good while I have repaid you with evil. Today you have crowned your goodness toward me since Yahweh has put me in your power yet you did not kill me.' "

David's son Solomon gives us another example of forgiveness. Adonijah had intrigued against Solomon. Then Solomon arrived on the scene and Adonijah ran to the temple for sanctuary. This was told to Solomon and he responded (1 Kings 1:52-53): " 'Should he bear himself honorably, not one hair of his shall fall to the ground; but if he is found malicious he shall die.' King Solomon then sent for him to be brought down from the altar; he came and did homage to King Solomon; Solomon said to him, 'Go to your house.' "

Nothing at all was said about the past.

In addition to the examples of forgiveness, the Old Testament gives us clear instructions about forgiving.

In Exodus 23:4-5 God tells his people how to treat their enemies:

"If you come on your enemy's ox or donkey going astray, you must lead it back to him. If you see the donkey of a man who hates you fallen under its load, instead of keeping out of his way, go to him and help him."

This is the message of God who himself forgives everyone and who readily helps all who ask.

Proverbs tells us how forgiveness makes us stronger,

better people (19:11): "A man's shrewdness shows in equanimity, his self-respect in overlooking an offense."

Further, in 24:17, we read, "Should your enemy fall, do not rejoice, when he stumbles do not let your heart exult."

And in 24:29, "Do not say, 'I will treat him as he has treated me; I will repay each man as he deserves.' "

And again in 25:21-22: "If your enemy is hungry, give him something to eat; if thirsty, something to drink. By this you heap red-hot coals on his head, and Yahweh will reward you."

All of these are recommendations to avoid what can only be called mean-spirited behavior. Our enemy is a human being, beloved of God, and worthy to be treated the way we would want to be treated. We are told we must follow God's own example, who never fails to forgive and help all.

Ecclesiastes tells us (7:21): "Pay no attention to tell-tales; you may hear that your servant has reviled you; your own heart knows how often you have reviled others."

Here the solution is very simple. When we hear what others have done, before getting angry or indignant with them, we need only remember that we too at one time or another have done the same things and are likewise in need of forgiveness.

The Old Testament makes it abundantly clear that the God who forgives all expects that kind of behavior from his people. The shining examples of the great heroes of the Old Testament were forgiving people. The way to live a happy human life is to live the life of forgiveness. We await only the human example of the God-Man as shown in the New Testament.

b. *The New Testament*

The New Testament is full of forgiveness. One of the
most significant aspects of Jesus' teachings about the Father
is that God is a most loving, a most forgiving Father. He
wants to forgive us. He welcomes us into his arms.

A corollary is that we, too, must forgive. And there is a
close connection between the way that God forgives us and
the way we forgive those who offend us.

When his disciples asked Jesus how to pray he gave
them this prayer (Matthew 6:9-13):

> "Our Father in heaven, may your name be
> held holy,
> your kingdom come, your will be done on earth
> as it is in heaven.
> Give us today our daily bread.
> And forgive us our debts,
> as we forgive those who are in debt to us.
> And do not put us to the test, but save us from
> the evil one."

He goes on to say (Matthew 6:14-15): "Yes, if you
forgive others their failings, your heavenly Father will forgive you yours, but if you do not forgive others, your Father
will not forgive your failings either."

Forgive us as we forgive. What a sobering thought. But
Jesus tells us the same thing at other times.

In Matthew 5:23-24, we read:

"So then, if you are bringing your offering to the altar
and there remember that your brother has something

against you, leave your offering there before the altar, go and be reconciled with your brother first, and then come back and present your offering."

Jesus tells us that in order to make our prayer or sacrifice acceptable to God, our hearts must be right with our fellow human beings.

He says further in Matthew 5:43-45:

"You have learned how it was said: You must love your neighbor and hate your enemy. But I say to you: love your enemies and pray for those who persecute you; in this way you will be sons of your Father in heaven, for he causes his sun to rise on bad men as well as good, and his rain to fall on honest and dishonest men alike."

We have perhaps heard these words so often that sometimes we don't really hear them. Can we imagine what it would have been like to hear these words for the first time? We are to love our enemies: not just tolerate them, but actually love them. Only a loving and forgiving God could demand such a thing.

But are there limits to forgiveness? That is what Peter asked in Matthew 18:21-22:

"Then Peter went up to him and said, 'Lord, how often must I forgive my brother if he wrongs me? As often as seven times?' Jesus answered, 'Not seven, I tell you, but seventy times seven.' "

And seventy times seven, the unlimited number, is precisely how often God forgives us.

In Matthew 18:23-35, we read the parable of the unforgiving debtor. Here we see a man who owed his master a huge sum, ten thousand talents. As he had no means of repaying, his loving master forgave him the debt. This same servant then went out and met a fellow servant who owed him one hundred denarii, a paltry amount. This man too had no way to repay, and begged forgiveness. But the servant would not consider it. His master heard of his behavior and was righteously angry with him. The connection between the constant forgiveness that God extends to us and the way we must forgive our neighbors is transparently clear.

Not only did Jesus tell us again and again to forgive, but he was ever ready to forgive. In Luke 7:36-50, we read of the woman who was a sinner. She came to Jesus when he was dining with the Pharisee and brought an alabaster jar of ointment. Without a word she washed Jesus' feet with her tears and wiped them with her hair. Then she kissed Jesus' feet and anointed them with ointment. The Pharisee was shocked, but Jesus spoke up for the woman.

" 'For this reason I tell you that her sins, her many sins, have been forgiven her, or she would not have shown such great love. It is the man who is forgiven little who shows little love.' Then he said to her, 'Your sins are forgiven.' Those who were with him at table began to say to themselves, 'Who is this man, that he even forgives sins?' But he said to the woman, 'Your faith has saved you; go in peace.' "

In Luke 15:11-32, we learn the beautiful story of the prodigal son and what a story it is. Who could forget the father who, when the son was still far off, saw him and was moved to pity?

"He ran to the boy, clasped him in his arms and kissed him tenderly. Then the son said, 'Father, I have sinned against heaven and against you. I no longer deserve to be called your son.' But the father said to his servants, 'Quick!

Bring out the best robe and put it on him; put a ring on his finger and sandals on his feet. Bring the calf we have been fattening, and kill it; we are going to have a celebration, because this son of mine was dead and has come back to life; he was lost and is found.'"

What a loving father this son has. What a loving Father we have!

But Jesus' best example of forgiveness was the one he set on the cross as he was dying. His enemies did not ask forgiveness; in fact, many jeered at him. But that did not matter. He said, "Father, forgive them; they do not know what they are doing" (Luke 23:34).

The early disciples were quick to understand this message of forgiveness. In Acts 7:60, we read of the death of the first martyr, Stephen:

"Then he knelt down and said aloud, 'Lord, do not hold this sin against them,' and with these words he fell asleep."

Paul repeated Jesus' advice in Romans 12:14, 17-19: "Bless those who persecute you; never curse them, bless them. . . . Never repay evil with evil but let everyone see that you are interested only in the highest ideals. Do all you can to live at peace with everyone. Never try to get revenge; leave that, my friends, to God's anger."

In 1 Corinthians 4:12-13, Paul tells how he tries to practice what he preaches: "When we are cursed, we answer with a blessing; when we are hounded, we put up with it; we are insulted and we answer politely."

In Ephesians 4:32, he says simply, "Be friends with one another, and kind, forgiving each other as readily as God forgave you in Christ."

In Colossians 3:13, he reiterates: "Bear with one

another; forgive each other as soon as a quarrel begins. The Lord has forgiven you; now you must do the same."

The Scriptures are clear on God's loving forgiveness and our own need also to forgive. Forgiveness becomes necessary for membership in God's kingdom. It is the basis for salvation.

As we are forgiven, so too must we forgive. The Christian community is to be both a forgiven and a forgiving community.

But Jesus did not say forgiveness was easy, nor did he or his disciples ever promise that misunderstandings or quarrels would never arise. As long as we are human beings, there will be difficulties. But Jesus did promise his grace and his help, and he is ever faithful to his promises.

3.

Who Must We Forgive?

Throughout our lives we have many persons to forgive. Some of these are persons we love and want to forgive. Others are very difficult to forgive. Still others we don't even think about forgiving, but they need forgiveness all the same.

Ourselves

The first persons we must learn to forgive are ourselves. This will come as a surprise to many people who wonder if they already love themselves too much to worry about forgiving themselves.

But truly most of us do not like ourselves. And we all have a backlog of experiences to work through before we can become comfortable with ourselves.

It is natural to love ourselves, to protect ourselves. The self-preservation instinct is strong and it does not only consist in saving ourselves from bodily danger. Yet we don't all like ourselves. Many of us have been brought up in a way that has made us dislike ourselves. In severe cases, we may even hate ourselves. Many of us have been told from the time we were children that we are not very good. Many of us had parents who were afraid that we might grow up into snobbish and proud persons so they refrained from telling us that we were smart or good-looking or capable. Or perhaps our parents thought that if we were told that our work was good, we would forever rest on our laurels. We were not given a good self-image. Many of us live in perpetual guilt and regret about things that often we could not have done any differently.

There are people who recall with regret embarrassing incidents that happened in their childhood. Perhaps they did something foolish at one time or another and their parents severely scolded them. Looking at the incident back through the years they are again embarrassed. They wish they could go back and change the situation. But of course that is not possible. Still the thought of the incident fills them with pain, and this for something that was merely foolish or involuntary on their part.

Others look back on incidents that they did fully voluntarily, incidents that they deeply regret now. Looking back as adults, they wonder how they could have been so selfish, so thoughtless, so mean or cruel. They see only the incident and do not remember their mindset at the time, the hurt they were enduring then, the narrow viewpoint, the strong peer pressure, or just the impetuousness of youth. As adults, they cannot now forgive this young person they used to be.

We could ask ourselves some questions. If this was someone else we were talking about, could we forgive that person? If we knew a child, a stranger's child, who had acted as we did, would we, could we, forgive that child? Of course we could. We would forgive easily and soon forget about the whole thing, especially if we knew how confused or uncertain the child was at the moment, or perhaps the pain that drove him to the unwelcome behavior. So too we must look at ourselves.

We may find it helpful to go back in our minds and forgive the child we once were. It would be good if we could look at ourselves in a picture at whatever age we choose and speak to that child. We need to express forgiveness and we need to extend a hug to the child we once were.

We then need to look at ourselves in a mirror. We are flawed human beings, even the best of us. Perhaps we are not beautiful or handsome, perhaps we have never been, but there is much to admire in every one of us. For every failure in our lives, there have been a multitude of successes. For each time we have been needlessly harsh with someone, there have been a million times when we have been kind or at least even-tempered. We are rarely fair with ourselves. We are rarely as kind to ourselves as we make efforts to be kind to others.

This is so true that when we are given compliments we often don't believe them. This has been called the Impostor Syndrome. We wonder how many compliments we would receive if people really knew us. And when we do not receive a compliment, when people find fault with us, there is something in us that is more likely to believe that than the compliments. Our Impostor Syndrome says, "Aha! These people have seen beneath the disguise and found the person we really are."

This explains what happens to a teacher, for example,

who, when, after having taught a class of twenty-five students, receives glowing evaluations from twenty-four of them, and one not-so-glowing report. This teacher may totally disregard the twenty-four beautiful comments ("Best teacher I ever had", "Would recommend this course to anyone!") and concentrate on the one derogatory report which may represent a disgruntled student more than a fair evaluation of the teacher.

There is another reason why we have so much difficulty forgiving ourselves. We often have built up an impossible ideal for ourselves. We would like to be perfect people, but every day we find that we are less than perfect. Each day we find ourselves saying, "I should," or, "I should have," "I could have, but I didn't." We are always falling short. This kind of thinking shows that we haven't quite accepted our human condition. We carry around with us much guilt because of our daily failings. But we are human beings and prone to imperfection. We need to love and accept ourselves just as we are.

This impossible ideal also often goes back to our childhood and the lack of praise we were given. But our parents were wrong. Giving us sincere compliments on our hard-earned achievements would not have made us proud and likely to rest on our laurels. It would have had the exact opposite effect. Our self-concept would have been strong and healthy and the effect would have been a freeing of our ability to accomplish. We would be less fearful, much happier persons. We would be able to ignore unfair criticism, and we would be able to profit from fair criticism without allowing it to damage us.

But we forgive our parents, too, for, as we shall see, they need much forgiveness.

Our Parents

Most of us have a love-hate relationship with our parents. At times one or the other emotion dominates, fortunately usually love. For at heart, most of us love our parents because most of our parents, in spite of all their mistakes, love us.

In a biological sense, anyone can be a parent. All one has to do is have a child. This does not teach anyone to do the right things in parenting.

Psychologists have argued for a long time whether or not human beings actually have any instincts the way animals do. At one time, mothering was considered instinctual behavior. But if that were true then all mothers would care for their children. But we know they do not. We have, in recent years, seen too many incidents of child neglect and abuse to imagine that every woman who has had a child automatically feels and acts toward it with tenderness.

Mothering, like most human behavior, is learned behavior. We learn to mother by being mothered. We learn to care for others by being around those who do. It is no surprise that parents who abuse their children often themselves had abusive parents.

It is also no surprise that parents make many mistakes with their children. Many parents learn only by being parents. When they have their first child, they are often young and inexperienced and they may worry too much. In addition they may be tired and overworked or they may be going through a difficult time financially or otherwise. As time goes on and they have other children, they may become too lenient. This is something most children are quick to notice and comment on.

On the other hand, each child is different. What worked with one child will not necessarily work with another. So even if parents seem to learn parenting with each child, there are always new lessons to learn.

And parents are human. Even if they know exactly what to do, they do not always do it. As children carry around loads of guilt that their parents put on them as children, so do many parents carry around guilt that their children gave them.

We need to forgive our parents. We need to recognize that they made many mistakes and forgive them. We also need to forgive things that were more than mistakes. Our parents were not saints and many of their rules were simply arbitrary and had no reason. Some parents were at times downright mean.

Some children have even more difficult deeds of their parents to forgive: the alcoholic parent, the parent who deserted the family, the cruel, mean parent, the parent who played favorites with the children, the selfish parent, the parent who gave the child no encouragement or support, the parent who refused to help the child when the child needed it most, and above all, the parent who refuses to forgive the child for his or her own behavior.

Fortunately, there is usually one underlying theme that makes forgiving parents possible. There is a real love that may be hidden under layers of anger and anguish and guilt, but it is there. And we can reach out to parents and forgive them.

We need to do this sometimes mentally many times

before we can bring ourselves to do it in actuality. But it can be done. Ultimately we want to get to know our parents better.

It is strange, often, how little we know our parents as people. We know them as our mother and father, but perhaps we do not know them as people. Many adults today who look back at their parents as people, not just as parents, will see people who were severely scarred by the Great Depression. Others will see frightened immigrants who, even after many years, found the United States a cold and forbidding country.

Younger persons who look back may see their parents as people who could never quite measure up to their own parents. Or they may see a mother and father who wanted so much to give their children a beautiful home, cars, education, travel, that they spent little time with them. Or they may simply see very ordinary people.

This last point is important. We never quite think of our parents as just ordinary people. As young children our parents are some kind of gods. They know all, they see all, they take care of all. Later, they at least can be counted on to take care of things and they know the answers to most questions.

The day comes, however, when we see they don't know the answers. We reach a point in our education when mom and dad cannot help us. Or we reach a point in our lives when we are sure they will never understand. We may well be right; they may not understand. And this is not a fault in them. They are just ordinary people.

Forgiveness of parents will free us of some of the sad memories we have of our childhood. It is not necessarily a good idea for us to go to our parents and forgive them in so many words. That may have the opposite effect we want: "But there is nothing to forgive! I was right!" And we are back again to arguing.

It is not important to establish who was right. What we want now is just to love each other and to forgive in such a way that we no longer bring up the bad times. Our forgiveness will show itself in the kind way we treat our parents, in the way we will ignore the past, in the way we will not try to make them suffer for the suffering they have given us.

Some children subconsciously cause their parents to suffer. They do things that hurt their parents, because they have been hurt. What they are forgetting is that they are hurting themselves more than they are hurting their parents. Instead of cooling water to put the fire out, they are pouring on gasoline.

It has been said that no one is ever fully mature until he has buried the pains and sufferings of his childhood. The sooner we forgive our parents, the sooner we will be able to live a full life as an adult.

Other important people in our lives

If one day we are in a grocery store and a stranger looks at us and at the grocery cart we have and says something like, "No wonder you are fat!" we may well be offended. And we may even give an angry retort. Many of us, however, are more likely simply to stare at that person. What right does a perfect stranger have to say such a thing to us?

But it is not hard to simply forget that incident. The

stranger means nothing to us. It is not a matter of holding a grudge; chances are we may never see that person again.

The situation is quite different when the insulting person is a member of our family or someone whom we had called a friend. Then we are deeply offended and do not forget the insult. We see the person too often. We have too much invested in that person to ignore him or her.

Thus, for the most part, it is not strangers that we must forgive. It is our friends or enemies, if the latter have entered our lives sufficiently to be called enemies.

It is very common for brothers and sisters to fight. The label "sibling rivalry" is well known because it is so common. Brothers and sisters are forced to be together and to share so many things that they both want. Fortunately most brothers and sisters play happily together as often as they fight. Fortunately as they mature the fighting brothers and sisters often become good friends. Or, if not good friends, at least supportive relatives. At times, however, this does not happen and sibling rivalry extends into adulthood. Sometimes it is only small incidents that break into full rifts, gathering as it were, all the accumulated pain since childhood. There are brothers and sisters who won't have anything to do with each other, who won't even attend a family party if the other is there.

But this is all so foolish. All is forgiveable. Sometimes what brothers and sisters need to do is get together and talk. Perhaps as adults with their own lives, their own spouses and children, their own accomplishments, they are now secure enough to talk. But this again does not always work. If it is too painful to bring up the past and exorcise the ghost, perhaps the ghost can be buried without opening the coffin.

Family members can get together and discuss neutral things. After a long time they are likely to find that they have much more in common than they thought.

This is true with other relatives and with others who have been a part of our lives. Occasionally two persons are good friends, but something happens in their friendship that destroys it and something in each of them. It may be a violation of a confidence. It may be the overstepping of the bounds of friendship. Whatever it is, the friendship may or may not be salvageable. What is important is that the two persons do not harden their hearts and close their minds to each other. At least in prayer, they should remember each other. At least in meeting they should be civil. At least in thought they should be kind.

Enemies

Most of us don't think we have any real enemies. But we can classify as an enemy anyone who has had a significant role in our lives in a way that has been deliberately harmful. If we are in a business in which a co-worker or competitor has deliberately tried to destroy us for his own gains or in some kind of revenge, he is an enemy. If we had a former friend who sets out to destroy our reputation she is an enemy. If we or someone in our family are mugged or raped or wounded by someone on the street, the one who hurt us is an enemy. These persons are much harder to forgive. They deliberately set out to hurt us. They did mean to hurt us.

How can we possibly forgive such persons? Our first reaction may be to want revenge. We may demand the death penalty for the drunk driver who killed our daughter. (He had been arrested three times before for drunk driving!) We may want the person to go to prison for life. We may want him to suffer the kinds of pain we have suffered. We may want him to go bankrupt in his own business.

But we need to look carefully at these feelings. Do they really satisfy? Is revenge really sweet? Ask persons who have gotten even, as they say. Revenge is not sweet. Revengeful persons feel an emptiness even if they have destroyed the other person. It has not given them back what they have lost either.

But it is very hard to forgive. We would not be able to do it at all if it were not for the example of Jesus. Even as he hung on the cross he forgave his enemies. He responded in kindness to those who were cruel to him.

Ultimately, of course, forgiveness is the only way — not just for the enemy, but for ourselves. What we do not want to imitate is the behavior that we find so reprehensible in the other.

The Circumstances of our Lives

Yes, we must forgive the circumstances of our lives. The circumstances of our lives are not chosen by us; we were placed where we were. Some of us blame God for this and we may find ourselves angry with God. Now some will wonder at this. How dare we be angry with God, how dare we imagine that God needs forgiveness? Surely he deserves from us love, trust, obedience, and acceptance. What he does is always right.

Of course that is true. But our minds are weak and our ideas of God are poor. Since we know God made us as we are, we wonder why he made us so weak and wavering. We wonder why he gave us the home and family he did; we could have done so much better elsewhere. We wonder why he allowed our spouse, or our child, or our best friend to die. We wonder why he allows disease and wars to go on unabated. We wonder why he treats us the way he does.

We need to forgive him in the sense that we need to forgive him in the image we have of him. He loves us more than we will ever know. He cares for us. He wants only what is good for us. But it often does not look that way to us. Our forgiveness of him is rather a begging of his forgiveness for painting him differently than he really is. We need to surrender to God. We need to believe that he will do the best for us.

4.

Methods of Forgiveness

How do we forgive? Forgiveness, like all graces, comes first from God. He forgives us constantly and it is he who will show us how to forgive and who will make forgiveness possible. His grace of forgiveness is given for the asking. This is a grace we should request every day.

We need daily to forgive. We cannot wait for others to come to us and ask forgiveness or to apologize. When they come we want to forgive them readily and whole-heartedly, but we will not be able to do this if we have not already mentally forgiven them. The following are a few suggested ways of practicing forgiveness.

1. *Prayerful Forgiveness*

This is a kind of mental prayer. You will need to find a quiet place and put yourself into this situation.

It is a beautiful day. You take a walk outside. The sun warms you, but it is not hot. There is a cooling breeze. You breathe deeply of the cool air. It feels good to expand your lungs.

You walk down a path among the trees. Ahead of you, you see someone, a person you recognize. The man you see before you has dark hair and olive skin and is wearing a robe and sandals. He is waiting for you.

It is Jesus. Breathlessly you walk up to him. He looks at you and smiles at you. It is clear that he is very pleased to see you.

You look into his eyes and you read the love he has for you. Guilt flicks into your mind, but his look wipes that away.

He takes your hand.

"Come," he says in his gentle warm voice that you feel you could never hear too much of, "come, there is someone you need to talk to."

"Who is it?" you ask.

"Someone who needs your forgiveness," he says, and then he names someone who has hurt you. It may be your mother, your father, a boss, a former friend. It may be yourself in a younger stage in your life.

As soon as you hear the name, you cringe.

He senses the cringe and turns to you.

"Don't worry," he says, "I will be with you. I will be with you every second."

"I am not sure I can forgive him (or her)," you say.

"Of course you can," he says. "And please *do* forgive him. Remember I love that person."

You almost mutter, "You sure love some weird people," but you don't, remembering that he loves you too, whom some other people might call weird.

You walk together through the trees hand in hand. It is so pleasant to be with him, so pleasant to be with someone who knows all about you and who loves you so much. His very presence makes your heart sing.

And then ahead of you under a tree you see the person you need to forgive. This person looks at you. Perhaps his look is one of fear; he may think you have come to take revenge. Or his look may be one of arrogance. Or he may not be able to even meet your eye.

You look at Jesus and then you go up to the person.

"I came to see you," you say, "because I want to forgive you. You have hurt me, I cannot deny that, and perhaps I have also hurt you. Now I want the two of us to forgive it all. I want to forgive you. I love you."

The person looks at you and you can see that he is listening, but perhaps he, too, is not yet ready to let go.

Jesus gives you a nudge.

You embrace the other person. You hug him and tell him you love him.

But Jesus has his arms around both of you and it is all right.

This method seems to work best when there are angers and hurts that go back for many years, perhaps into our childhood. It also works best with persons whom we can no longer personally tell that we forgive them: parents or others who have died. And it is the very best for forgiving ourselves. If we could picture ourselves as we were at age 10 or age 16 or the period of our lives when our behavior was not what we wish it had been, we could forgive ourselves. Imagine the young person we were, so lonely, so lost, so hurting, that we did the things we did. One thing we must always remember. If that person were someone else, someone else's child at age 10, 16, or whatever, we would certainly forgive. Why do we find it so much easier to be kind to others than we are to ourselves?

2. *Letter Forgiveness*

The one thing we never want to do is to simply break off from someone else. Even hatred is closer to love than complete indifference is. The family whose members fight at least are aware of each other's presence. The family members who live far apart and do not even tell others where they are, nor express any interest in what is happening to each other, are the hardest to reach.

An image may help. We all have many bonds to other human beings and we need those bonds. Without them our lives would be totally unhappy. Picture, for human beings, a large group of pods in a box, each one separate in itself, but with many little threads reaching out to others. Some will have strong bonds to only one or two other people. Some will have strong bonds to many many people. A few will have simply their own bonds tied tightly around themselves.

For our image let us imagine that the bonds are red when they represent warm and supportive bonds, but blue when they are destructive. When a person is totally tied in his own bonds, they are mostly blue. But there are blue bonds among other people as well.

As we work with this imagery, we learn that it is possible

to change blue to red relatively easily, but very difficult to build new bonds where old ones have died. And dead bonds are found among the live ones.

We don't want to drive people away nor do we want to be driven away. We may not yet be able to forgive a hurt, but we don't want to lose contact.

For some people, personal visits and even phone calls are too painful. We find ourselves yelling at the other person and digging deeper wounds instead of healing those that are there.

Or the personal visits may not be possible because the person has left the area, or long distance phone calls may simply be too expensive. Letters help.

Anyone who has ever tried this will know how valuable letters are. I am not speaking of letters that constantly reiterate the pain that has been caused. Nor am I talking about letters that keep giving or asking forgiveness. I am talking about simple, warm, friendly letters. These letters, no matter what they are saying about the weather and the activities of one's family, are saying over and over again, "I care about you. I want you to know I care about you. Our love is not dead. It may not be as strong now, but it is not dead."

Perhaps Christmas or birthday cards are a start. These don't require much writing. And then perhaps little notes, little messages. This person is still important.

But, someone will ask, what if the response is nasty letters? I recommend that these be ignored. Write as if you didn't recognize the nastiness.

And what if there is no answer at all? Keep at it. It may take years, but these letters will keep the person in touch.

3. *Slowly coming together*

Sometimes you want to get together with the person, but it is too hard for both of you. You have determined that you will not break off, but a simple talking of the mutual disagreement is still too painful for both of you. There are ways you can gradually get together.

a. Invite the person to a party with a routine invitation. This shows that you consider him or her still part of your group. At times it may be useful to add on the invitation, "I really hope you can make it."

b. Call the person and tell him some family information. Someone else could make the call, but you want to make it to give you the chance to talk to him. Perhaps you will not say more than what is required for the information, but you will have made a contact.

c. Visit your mother or someone at a time when you know the person you have had a falling-out with will be there. Unless that person will make things unpleasant for your parent or friend, this is a good time. It takes the pressure off both of you to have a mutual loved one present. You may not even talk much to each other, but you are sharing a visit.

d. Shop at the same grocery store or some such place so that you see each other. Smile and go about your work. This again is contact.

e. Keep on sending gifts to the person's children or others who could expect a gift from you. Again, you are avoiding any kind of breaking off.

f. Hold the next family party at your house so that there will be a built-in reason for the person to come. An added benefit is that few people are willing to be unpleasant to each other in someone's own house. One is not to be unpleasant to one's guest.

At first you will not be able to talk about much except the most innocuous subjects. But there will be a time when you can laugh together over a joke, or cry together when a family member dies. There may be a time when you find yourself in the kitchen with your friend/enemy washing the dishes. You may find yourself playing a game with him or her.

Come together slowly and take your time. Here, as elsewhere, patience pays off.

There is an old saying that time heals all wounds, and it does indeed. But we can help time by giving it the opportunity. And wounds will heal.

4. *Confrontation*

Forgiveness requires great sensitivity and tact. Saying too much is just as bad as saying too little. There is often a time when a direct confrontation is necessary. But the word confrontation should not be construed to mean a straight-from-the-shoulder facing down of another person. Rather it will be a loving meeting where two persons who love each other want to solve their difficulties.

It is important that this meeting be prepared for with prayer. The one planning the meeting should decide exactly what he or she will say and then trust to the Holy Spirit to make the words come out right. In addition, the one planning it should be aware that although he or she has thought things out and carefully prepared, the other may not have. This will put the other at a distinct disadvantage. One needs to approach things slowly and with tact.

The situation should be one where you will not be interrupted. It should not be a place which reminds both of you of ancient conflicts. It should be somewhere mutually acceptable. Then, calmly and quietly, you may wish to say something like this:

"I am very concerned about what has happened between us. I don't want it to be like this. I know that if we put our heads together we can work this out. I hope you want it as much as I do."

The response may be less enthusiastic than you expect, but at times it will be more. Often the other person has been wanting to patch things up, but has been unwilling to take the first step. At other times, you may get a response that goes something like this:

"Well, if you are willing to admit you're wrong, I will accept your apology."

Here is an impasse. What if you are quite sure you are not wrong? At that point you can say something like:

"I did not come here to assign wrong or right or anything like that. I came here to be your friend again. But I am quite willing to apologize for anything that I have done that has offended you. We don't have to agree on everything, but that should not change our friendship."

Notice how difficult this kind of confrontation is. Yet there are times when it should be used. It may be exactly what is needed to clear the air.

A couple of warnings are in place, however:

— Concentrate only on the disagreement that has arisen between you. Do not drag up incidents that happened years ago. Do not analyze each other's personalities or their flaws. Talk about the issue at hand only.

— Once this confrontation is completed, it should not be repeated. When it is over, it is over. And it should be confidential. It is not necessary to tell others all about it.

5.

Effects of Forgiving and Not Forgiving

Lack of Forgiveness

Perhaps first it is necessary to talk about what lack of forgiveness does. We speak of being hurt by others. Sometimes this hurt is physical as, for example, when through the carelessness or even evil of others, they have wounded us or caused us physical pain. Those are real hurts and we are very much aware of them. More often, however, the wound is psychological. This type of wound does not scar the body but it does scar the soul. Each time we are wounded physically or psychologically we have a sore, first an open one, then a scab. Eventually if we do not pick at the scab, a scar may appear, but even that, in time, may disappear.

But let us look first at the open sore. It is terrible. Every time we see the sore, hurting and bleeding as it is, we suffer all over again. The pain is deep and cannot be ignored. It is cruel and foolish when someone is hurt to say simply, "Forget about it."

The hurt person cannot forget the open sore on his body or soul.

What needs to be said is something like this: "Let me help you put some healing medicine on it."

And then we can help the person heal.

Unfortunately, however, too many persons do not allow themselves to heal. They do not apply healing medicine. They let the wound bleed. They may even suffer loss of blood from a wound that could easily have been covered.

This happens psychologically when people continue to dwell on their pain. They may tell everyone they meet about their suffering. They may plan revenge or they may hurt others who happen to get in their way. Or they may continually expose their wound so that it gets hurt again, in the manner of the one who refuses to cover a wound so that the wound is torn open time and again.

Later when the wound starts to heal, some people insist on opening it again. Even many years later, some people will not allow their wounds to heal. I have met people who talk about the way they were treated by, for example, their husband or wife or their parents. They were indeed mistreated. When asked when this occurred the answer may be "Twenty-seven years ago."

And they are still nursing the wound.

When we refuse to forgive, we keep the wound festering. And the result of the festering wound of the soul is exactly the same as that of the body. The scar is there, disfiguring one. But the scar is on the one who does not forgive. There may be no scars on the unforgiven one, especially if he or she is far away and never has contact with those who were wounded, especially if he or she doesn't even know the pain they've caused.

Make no mistake about it. The scar does disfigure a person. One who carries around grudges closes off a part of his heart to others. Sometimes he closes off such a large part of his heart that he is unable to show anyone else any kindness. He is in effect saying, "Never again will anyone hurt me."

But he is also saying, "Never again will anyone love me." And, "Never again will I love anyone."

The person who refuses to forgive is swallowing a deadly bitter potion. The more one takes in the bitterness, the more it affects one's whole personality. And the more one allows one's life to be shadowed by someone else, the more bitter does one become.

When we refuse to forgive, we allow the persons who have hurt us too much power over us. They have hurt us and have gone and we may never see them again, but we allow them to continue to hurt us day after day. We allow them to destroy our happiness and even the happiness of those around us. We hate them for what they have done to us, we say, but ultimately we are allowing them to continue the effects of what they have done.

I am not saying that forgiving is easy; I *am* saying it is possible. I am also saying that it is wise; it is sensible; it is for our own good.

If we cannot forgive for the sake of the other, we should certainly be able to forgive for ourselves. We are ultimately the ones who feel the effects of forgiveness.

Effects on the Forgiver

So what good does it do for the forgiver? When we empty ourselves of bitterness and anger, we are letting the dark poison out of our system. In the Middle Ages people had the idea that if you were ill, it was because there was bad blood in you. It had to be let out. To do that they literally bled people, cutting them and allowing the blood to flow out. Now, stories have come down to us of persons who died or nearly died because of bleeding. But interestingly enough, there are also many stories of people who were bled, fell into a deep sleep, and were much improved the next day.

Forgiving others can be very much a blood-letting. It is painful and we think we are losing something we need and want. It is hard for us to let go of anger and resentment. We feel we have a right to that anger, and probably we do. But slowly we learn that it is a virus in us, it is bad blood in us, that is destroying us. When we have made the painful effort to let go of our anger and even hatred, we find ourselves exhausted. This is because letting go of bitterness takes a huge amount of emotional energy. We too may fall into a deep sleep. I recommend that in the act of forgiveness we be kind to ourselves too. Perhaps at this time we need more rest, long relaxing warm baths, our favorite easy chair, a glass of wine. When it is over, we start to improve. The hurt has gone and the wound will now heal. We will become whole persons.

As when we keep the anger inside us, the bitterness tends to poison our whole system, destroying our happiness and the way we treat others, so too when we forgive sweet forgiveness sweeps through our whole system. It makes us kinder to ourselves, for, after all, we have much to forgive ourselves, too.

It makes us sweeter to those around us. And the day will come when we will even be kind to our enemies.

Forgiveness puts us at peace with ourselves and with others. Part of the Easter message that Jesus came to give us was Peace:

"Peace be with you," he said, and then he went on to say:

"Receive the Holy Spirit. For those whose sins you forgive, they are forgiven; for those whose sins you retain, they are retained" (John 20:21, 23).

We are accustomed to thinking of these words as pertaining to the Sacrament of Penance as they no doubt do. But all of us are also to forgive others. And when we forgive, we extend peace to those who have hurt us as well as peace to ourselves. Persons who complain that they are not at peace with themselves need to look at the forgiveness they extend in their lives. There is nothing so giving of peace as forgiveness.

Furthermore, when we forgive and have been forgiven, we learn compassion. We are now able to understand why people act the way they do and to suffer the pain they endure with them. This is what compassion means, and truly one who has never suffered is not able to feel compassion for anyone. We become tolerant of others, less willing to find fault, more willing to reach out to others in their needs.

Effects on the Forgiven and Unforgiven

As we have seen, perhaps the one who has offended does not even know about the pain he has caused others. And there *are* some who do not. There are others, perhaps ourselves included, who know the pain when a loved one will not forgive us. Perhaps we would like to mend the separation that a disagreement or misunderstanding or even a downright meanness on our part has caused. But someone else will not forgive us, perhaps will not even talk to us. We may even have humbly asked forgiveness only to have the other person refuse it. Or, to refuse it a more subtle way, such as happens when one says, "I forgive you," but in his actions shows that he has not. Or says, "I forgive you, but I can never trust you again." Or, "I forgive you but I cannot forget what you did." Or, "I forgive, but just stay out of my way." Or while saying he forgives deliberately hurts us.

These are very painful situations. We cannot get into the other person's mind or heart. We cannot change his mind. There is little we can do except to extend our own forgiveness to that other person.

It is strange how misunderstandings seem to take on a life of their own. Sometimes they grow and grow until they are a veritable though invisible wall between two people. And all we can do is bang our head against the wall.

The unforgiven person who asks forgiveness does indeed suffer.

So does the unforgiven person who does not ask forgiveness. He carries around with him the fact that he has hurt others and it is unresolved. There is a strange psychic energy that operates between people. We have all witnessed love that was so obvious we could almost touch it. And we have seen hatred that frightened us with its evil power even when it was not directed toward us. The same is true of forgiveness and lack of it. They are powers that touch the other human person.

A friend of mine gave me an interesting thought one day. We were discussing a rather notorious criminal whose story was in the newspaper. He was hardened with little thought of the value of other person's lives.

"Look at that," she said, "he will not change. He cannot change until someone forgives him. While we all look at him appalled and without compassion, he cannot change. He needs forgiveness."

And I think she was right.

As forgiving sets us free, so does being forgiven. Forgiveness gives us peace and life and our own personal resurrection.

All people need forgiveness. We need it as much as we need to give it. It, along with its stronger sister love, are the most powerful weapons in the world.

Some people seem to think that hate is strong, the way, in many stories, the devil seems so strong. In these stories one prays to God for years and the good life eludes him. Then he makes contact with the devil and immediately all good things come to him. If he is lucky, on his deathbed, he reneges on his bargain with Satan. But such stories are all false. The devil is not more powerful than God nor can he give us the good things of life more than God can.

It is God who loves us. It is also God who gives us all good things. The devil only knows how to give anger and hatred and sorrow and pain. Only God gives us love and gentleness and compassion. Only God knows how to teach us to forgive. He should be able to do that since he is a master at it himself; he does it often enough.

6.

Ten Things Always To Do

1. Pray. The grace of forgiveness comes from God and he will give it to us if we ask for it.

Pray every day for forgiveness of all that we have done that has offended God or others. This will put us into the mindset of praying for our enemies.

Pray for those who have hurt you. Pray for them every day. Ask God to help you cope with them. Think of all the good things you would like to happen to these persons and pray that they will happen. Pray for forgiveness. Pray that the persons who have hurt you will change or at least that they will no longer hurt you. If you cannot honestly pray for those persons' own good then at least pray that they will stop hurting you. Or if not even that, then pray for the desire to forgive. Forgive if you can, pray to forgive if you can't, and finally, if even that doesn't help, pray for the desire to forgive.

And it is not out of place to say this prayer in extreme emergencies: "God, this person has hurt me deeply. I want to forgive him, but right now I am feeling great pain and anguish and anger. I am afraid that if I see him right now, I shall respond to him angrily, perhaps say or do things that I will regret. So, please, keep him out of my way!"

2. Try to understand why the one who has hurt you acted as he did. There is an old saying that to understand all is to forgive all. This saying is usually true, but it will take us some effort to understand. Such understanding, however, does not usually come from questions to the person such as this: "Why did you do this?" Such questions do not really want an explanation; they are a reproach. It is also true that many people do not even know the reasons why they do things.

But we can think about the person and see why. Sometimes in family members there are reasons with a long history. Perhaps the mother's father or brother died from acute alcoholism. For a child of hers to even take a drink immediately makes her think that the child is following in those footsteps. Or someone may be suffering from loneliness or failure or suffering of some kind and this makes him act the way he does. Even illness can bring on a chemical change that causes, in some people, unwelcome behavior.

It is often easier to understand behavior which does not affect us personally than it is to comprehend that which touches us. We need to take a detached view of that person's behavior, as if we were explaining a stranger's behavior to someone else.

As we realize why some people act the way they do, we do not find their behavior excusable, but we do understand it better. Surely a parent should not take his anger out on a child when his boss has yelled at him. That behavior is not appropriate, but it is understandable.

There will be times when we simply cannot understand another's behavior. It seems totally out of line. In those instances, above all, there is a reason. Usually later we will find out what the reason is. Once we understand, we are closer to being able to forgive.

3. Remember your own failings and weaknesses. We all need forgiveness. We have certainly experienced the forgiveness from other people that we are now required to give to someone else. What if other people held against us all the things we have done to others through the years? Most of us, if we think about it, realize that others have endured much from us and still love us. Remembering that will help us to avoid the approach that some people take when they say that others should understand their behavior and forgive it, but they find it difficult to do so for them. That is too uncomfortably close to the story in the Scriptures of the unforgiving servant.

4. Smile at the person who has hurt you. A smile costs very little and means so much, it has often been said. But people who are trying to forgive know that a smile is often difficult. There is something in us that does not want to let go of our pain. We want that pain to be apparent to the one who hurt us. For us to smile and act as if nothing happened means that we have passed over the pain.

In truth the pain may still be there. The smile will not only lessen the pain, but it will help us to get closer to forgiveness. The first smile may be difficult, but it gets easier in time.

5. Be especially kind to others. As we have seen, when we are hurt the tendency is to lash out at others. This is not only counter-productive, but continues the chain of hurt. Since we have been hurt, our attitude should not be that we then want to hurt others, but that we do not want to give to others what has been given to us. We do not want to pass on to others what we ourselves have found so reprehensible.

It is also not the time to withdraw from others, to crawl in our shells and nurse our hurt. It is time for us to loosen ourselves and give of ourselves to others.

6. Ask a favor of the one who has hurt you. Long ago a wise old woman advised this. If you have been hurt, she said, one of the best ways to forgive is not to do something for the person who has hurt you, but to ask him to do something for you. This does not always work, but it is psychologically sound. It says to that other person several things: I have not cut you off nor do I think you want to cut me off. I think you will want to do this for me. I am not too proud to ask for your help. I want to let bygones be bygones.

7. Forgive mentally. It is important to do this first before doing it verbally. We may find that we must do it many many times mentally before it rings true to us. Psychologists today talk much about imaging and the power of imagination. In such imaging, we are told to mentally rehearse something we must do that is difficult to do. They give such examples as performing in public, giving a speech, or speaking to a difficult client. It should also be used to rehearse our forgiving and to make it sound sincere. When someone asks us to forgive, we are taken off guard. But if the

request for forgiveness sounds insincere, even sarcastic, we are only more angry.

8. Forgive verbally. This does not necessarily need to be in the simple terms, "I forgive you." Sometimes the response to this statement is an angry "There's nothing to forgive!" for if extending forgiveness is hard, so is accepting it. Often the message of forgiveness is simply quietly reestablishing relations. We talk to each other as friends. We do not insult and hurt that person. We try to be friendly and warm as usual.

Or we may sit down and talk a long time with the person. In the course of the conversation we may bring up the disagreement and talk about it. But we express it in terms like this:

"I thought about our conversation yesterday, and I have been feeling very upset about it. I value your friendship and do not want anything like this to stand between us."

Perhaps you need to express the fact that you cannot see eye to eye with this person on the issue involved. But there are so many issues you do agree on, that this one should not destroy your relationship.

For some people it is necessary simply to call a truce. The issue will never again be discussed, but you will be friends.

However this is handled, and it takes real skill to handle it well, it is important not to say too much. Remember that the wounds are still tender and better not be touched much. Years later when the wounds have thoroughly healed you may be able to really talk about it. But take your time.

9. Accept offers of forgiveness. We all know how difficult it is to ask forgiveness. Certainly it should not be so hard to extend forgiveness when it is offered. However, many people find it so. They do not want to let the other person off the hook. Yet there are few things in the Scriptures which are more explicit.

"How often shall I forgive my brother? Seven times?"

"Seventy times seven," Jesus says.

And we have his own example. He never refuses to forgive us.

Now some will say, "That is all well and good, but how can we allow people just to walk all over us when we know well that they are most likely to repeat their unacceptable behavior?"

We can forgive anyway. Perhaps the reason they do not improve is that they have not really thought out how to improve. It is like the person who wants to quit smoking. He tries and fails. He feels guilty and resolves to try again. But he is likely to fail again if he does nothing other than resolve to quit. He needs to plan some other changes in his life that will help him to change.

Perhaps we can help the people who continually fail. Perhaps they need reminders of their behavior. But one thing is certain: we never want to harden our hearts against anyone who sincerely asks forgiveness. And, just like the smoker who fails 17 times to quit, he may succeed the 18th. The fact that he asks forgiveness is the sign that he has not given up, that he has not stopped caring.

10. Enjoy your life. Dwell on the good things of life.

Be happy with your friends. Inhale deeply the fresh air. Look at the glorious sunshine. Appreciate the gently falling rain. All of these things will show how you have overcome anger and hatred, resentment and lack of forgiveness. You have rejected the poison. You have allowed yourself to be happy. And for sure, as Abraham Lincoln said, people are just about as happy as they have determined to be.

7.

Ten Things Never To Do

As there are some things we should always do to insure that we will be forgiving persons, there are others that we should never do. These actions work in the opposite direction; they make forgiveness all the more difficult and require that we undo them in the future.

1. Never say angry words you will regret. This is *very* difficult to do. When we are hurt the words come easily to our lips. But we must hold them back. That old rule about counting to ten before saying something is still a good rule. Maybe it should be counting to 100. Maybe it should be counting as far as we know how to count. Angry words take on a life of their own and go walking away, as has been said, on heavy boots. They step on other people. They also come back and step on us.

Since at the moment when we are hurt we do not usually have sufficient presence of mind to weigh what we say, we would do well to say very little. Perhaps nothing at all. There will be plenty of time later to say things. Plenty of time to think about the other's angry words or actions, as we shall certainly do.

2. Never never write angry words to anyone. If angry words which cannot be recalled go off and hurt others, imagine how harmful written words are. Angry spoken words are in the wind; they can be forgotten. In time they tend to dissipate. We may even forget exactly what was said.

Angry written words are for all time on paper. They can be read again and again, and often they are. Each time they are read, the sword in the wound sinks in deeper.

If you feel that you absolutely must write an angry letter, then do so. Write every angry thing you can think. Call the person every hateful name. Tell them of the horrible revenge you would like to wreak on them. Then take the paper and tear it up and burn it. But be sure to really burn it. It is so important never to write angry letters or notes. These angry written words are like nuclear weapons which can be buried in the earth but they still retain their potency.

3. Don't spend your time rehashing the argument, disagreement, or hurt. Don't spend your time telling everyone about it. Don't go over and over and over it. This kind of behavior is like rubbing salt in the wounds — your own wounds! Let go of it. Put a bandaid on the wound and stop looking at it. The more you think about and talk about your pain the more likely you will continue to feel the pain.

It may be necessary for you to share your hurt with a trusted friend. But you don't need to tell him about it every day. And you don't need to tell twenty friends about it. If your friends are real friends they will not pick at the scab; instead they will give you healing medicine.

4. Don't plan revenge. There are those who have

adopted as their motto: "Don't get mad; get even." This is childish and foolish. What does it mean to get even? For these people it means if I have been hurt, I shall hurt back, even in greater measure. But it will never stop there. When you hurt someone back, that person is most likely to start looking for another chance to get back at you. And the cycle will grow. "Vengeance is mine," says the Lord in the Bible. But as we well know, God is not out for revenge. He would rather heal both of us than hurt either of us.

5. Don't pick on others because you have been hurt. There is the old cartoon: The boss yells at the man; he yells at his wife; she yells at the child; the child kicks the dog. Each one is taking out his anger on someone who does not deserve it.

Often people who are weaker than the person who has hurt them take out their hurt and anger on someone else. They are in a position where they cannot strike back at the person who offended them, so they lash out at others. And often it is the persons we should most not hurt, members of our family. Sometimes it is strangers. One is hurt, the phone rings, and the person calling gets a surprisingly angry response.

We need to learn to channel our anger and hurt in other ways. The most harmful use of it is to hurt other innocent persons.

6. Don't try to kill with kindness in such a way that it is clear you are trying to build up guilt in the other person. Such behavior on the surface is at least not so harmful as lashing out or as hurting innocent people. But it is often perceived as totally insincere.

We human beings are interesting creatures. We are always reading messages that people are sending us even as they speak other words.

Someone has offended me. I make it a point to do all kinds of good things for him but I have in no way forgiven him. He understands that very well. My kind acts are poisoned and he tastes the poison. Far better for the two of us to have an open conversation and treat each other as whole normal human beings, flawed but forgiven.

7. Don't run away from the problem. Some people who have been hurt just try to run away from it. They may drop out of an organization if they think an officer of the organization has hurt them. How many Catholics are there who no longer go to church because the pastor was unkind to them. How many people have taken their children out of Catholic schools because a certain teacher hurt their feelings. How foolish these actions are! Who are they hurting? And are these actions likely to solve the problem? We all know that we never solve problems by running away from them. We should especially know that running away from a hurtful person will not help forgiveness.

8. Don't stop speaking to anyone ever! There are families in which, when they are quarreling, members simply refuse to talk to each other. A husband and wife will perhaps only communicate through their children. There are adult brothers and sisters who have not spoken to each other for years. One will not even attend a family party if the other is there.

There are many reasons for anger in a family. As we have seen, strangers and enemies do not have power to hurt us the way family members do. But the bonds of family are far too strong to be broken by lack of forgiveness. In a family, as nowhere else, lack of forgiveness works havoc. It can make one very unhappy for years. It can also make it hard for one's children to establish the relationships that should exist in the family.

9. Don't spend hours of precious time analyzing again and again what went wrong. Some people go into therapy for years with a psychologist in which they analyze again and again what happened in the past. Such therapy is only half the battle and the least important part. Look at the hurt, face it, see whether there is more than one side of it. Instead of concentrating on the hurt, concentrate on the pain of the person who inflicted the hurt. How often it happens that when we look at ourselves from the other person's viewpoint, forgiveness comes much easier. For, make no mistake about it, they too are suffering people.

10. Don't allow anyone else to be in charge of your happiness. Even the most hateful persons should not be allowed to destroy us, and they can destroy us only with our permission. When Viktor Frankl was in a concentration camp, he was deprived of everything. They took away his wealth, his position, his family, even his clothes and personal possessions. But he realized that they could never take away his right to his own attitude. He could become bitter or he could retain his integrity. This lesson that he learned under the most adverse circumstances is a valuable one for all of us today in our very ordinary circumstances. No one but ourselves can determine what kind of person we are or will be.

8.

Sacramental Forgiveness

Human forgiveness is wonderful to behold. We acknowledge that we have offended another and he/she forgives us, says to us in so many words, "That's all right, forget it."

And then proceeds to treat us as though nothing had ever happened. The offense is never brought up and if we ever bring it up, we are cut off shortly.

"That's over and done with. That was yesterday. This is today."

What a wonderful thing forgiveness is and how it can change the world. But forgiveness from human beings is not enough. We have also, we know well, offended God and we go to him and tell him we are sorry. How nice, we think, if he would personally tell us, "Forget it, it is over!"

When Jesus established his Church, he was well aware of the need we have to have personal, intimate, tactile contact with him. Those who had the privilege of sharing his life along the dusty roads of Galilee rejoiced in his presence. His simply being there changed everything for them. Their hearts burned within them, while he was with them.

But it was not his plan nor the plan of his Father that he

should stay forever. He was to return to his Father, but his Church would take his place while he was gone. And knowing our need for physical contact, he left us the sacraments.

Catholics who have been brought up in the Church often fail to recognize what marvels the sacraments are, how they are tangible signs of God's living and working among us. But that is precisely what they are; they make the invisible visible to us.

The Sacrament of Penance or Reconciliation is a case in point. At the present time it is going through a re-evaluation on the part of many Catholics. Many older Catholics will recall the long lines that used to be found outside the confessional on Saturday nights, the whispered list of sins on the part of the penitents, the hurried admonitions from the priest along with the assigned penance, and the dismissal from the confessional with the loud moving of the sliding door. Sad to say, for many this became a mere matter of routine.

Today people go to confession less frequently, but perhaps much more meaningfully. This sacrament, much less hurried today, gives us the opportunity to speak to God about our sins and failings, tell the priest acting for God of them, and then, wonder of wonders, hear the priest tell us also in God's name that they are forgiven. "Though your sins be as scarlet, they shall be white as wool."

All is forgiven. God tells us himself. What a wonderful gift this is from our Savior. No wonder that when he instituted it, he preceded his gift with the simple but profound words, "Peace be with you."

Not only is this a great consolation for many people, but

it is psychologically sound and healthy. The Sacrament of Reconciliation requires us to confess our sins, to admit them, to state them just as they are, without excuse or elaboration or exaggeration. We sometimes do not know how rare it is for us to do this, even to ourselves. Our self-love offers excuses, our sense of the dramatic wants to make our sins at least unusual or interesting. But in confession we tell them just as they are. This total honesty is itself balm for the soul.

Further, the need to tell another person, admit to another human being that we are sinners, is good for us. The monster within comes out in confession. As we all have experienced, what we had once so feared, our inner evil, comes out tamed and cured in the telling.

And then the priest, in God's name, forgives us. It is all over. We are wiped clean. We have only to accept God's gift of this sacrament and believe in it.

For this sacrament, like all sacraments, is a matter of faith. There is no magic here. The priest has no magic power, no control over God's grace. God gave us this sacrament. We believe in his working through it, and as long as we use it as he intended it, he promised to give us his grace. The priest is only the instrument, but a very necessary one.

What a joy this sacrament can be.

In the past there were those who found the sacrament burdensome, worried as they were about all their sins. Today we are more likely to find people who have lost their sense of sin. They may wonder, since they do not find themselves guilty of horrendous sins, what they have to confess in the sacrament. And yet these same persons often feel a deep sense of guilt or unrest. They too need to un-

burden their souls. They need to rethink what their actions
do to other people.

That is one of the wonderful aspects of the newly restored communal penance ritual. This form of penance is
supplemental to the personal confession, but it has aspects
to it that were much lacking in the past. By our sins we not
only have offended God, but we have damaged the Body of
Christ. We have shredded the bonds holding us together.
Our sins are never really just personal; they are also communal as our penance must be.

It has been said that in pre-Vatican II days we had a very
personalistic morality, a Jesus-and-I spirituality. We were to
save our own souls individually. Each of us needed to find
our own way to God.

That is indeed true, but what was not said was that we
did not venture on this trip alone. We were and are part of a
whole. We are the People of God. We worship together. We
help each other. We inspire each other. And we hurt and
hinder each other too. Thus if our sins have caused division
in the Church, our unity must be restored also in community. We need to get together as *sinners*, for such we are.

It is quite a sight to see a large parish gathered together
for a penitential service. We come admitting we have sinned
and are sinners and are in need of forgiveness. We need
forgiveness of each other and forgiveness of God. We need
to mend the fences and build the bridges that have been
damaged in our community.

After the community prayers and community examina-
tion of conscience, we make our own private confession.
Here we tell the priest — who is acting in the name of God
and representing the Church, our community — our sins

and express our sorrow. We are forgiven, we are told. All is forgiven.

We leave renewed, at peace with God, but also at peace with our fellowmen. The Sacrament of Penance is thus one of the greatest inducements we have to reach out to others and forgive them too. Knowing that we have been forgiven helps us to forgive others. We cannot, like the unjust servant, leave the presence of the Master who has just forgiven us everything, and then refuse to forgive our fellowman over the trifling offense he has committed against us.

Often the greatest burden that we take to the confessional with us is not our need of forgiveness, but our need to forgive. This is often the greatest grace we will receive from the sacrament, one that is heightened by the practice of communal penance. As the priest is God's minister sacramentally, we too share this in our forgiving of each other. We too stand in for God in our act of forgiveness.

II.

Related Issues

9.

Sorrow

When we ask forgiveness of others we express that we are sorry. We tell God that we are sorry when we have done wrong.

We also talk about being sorry when something happens to someone else. When the father of a friend dies, we may say, "I'm so sorry!"

Just what is sorrow? Is it sadness? Is it regret?

Sorrow is a much stronger emotion than regret and may or may not include sadness. Regret refers to the fact that we wish something could be undone. Or we would like to change something we did. It does not necessarily include sadness and certainly it may have nothing to do with forgiveness.

For example, one might say, "I regret now I didn't invest my money when the bank was paying 12% dividends."

Here hindsight tells us we made a mistake. But this is not sorrow or sadness.

Sorrow refers to a deep mental anguish we may feel over something that has happened. There is a strong sense of loss in sorrow. It seems to be closely related to sadness, a feeling of mourning or low-spirits.

Now, when we talk about being sorry and asking forgiveness, are we expected to be sorrowful or sad persons?

No one will quite believe us if we ask forgiveness from another and we do not in any way express any regret or sorrow over what we have done. Our asking for forgiveness will not seem sincere. The person who has been offended has been hurt and he wants us at least to be aware of the pain we have caused. He wants us to feel a little of that pain ourselves. So we should show and feel sorrow.

But this should not make us morbid persons.

On the level at which we communicate with God, we will truly feel sorrow for our offenses, but once we have been forgiven, we will be joyful persons, confident in his forgiveness. It would show a strange trust in God if we continued as though we were not forgiven, as though God himself did not take the burden from us.

When it comes to giving and receiving forgiveness from one another, it is more difficult. Just as people may not quite believe we are sincere if we do not express and show sorrow when we ask forgiveness, afterwards they may think it is not quite appropriate for us immediately to be happy, joyful persons. Somehow, we are supposed to wear our penitent robes for a while.

This is part of the difficulty of forgiving. We may need to wait a while before we start acting as if nothing has happened. But, when we ourselves forgive, we want to use as a model the forgiveness of God. We will not be so mean-spirited as to expect constant penitence. We will welcome the person back into our friendship.

10.

Guilt

One of the reasons that forgiveness is so important to us is that we all carry around with us much guilt. We have guilt from our childhood, guilt from our teenage years, and guilt as an adult. Our parents put guilt on us and we in turn put it on our children. Our children reciprocate by putting guilt on us too.

Now it is important to remember that guilt is not necessarily a bad thing. If we do not read certain psychologists carefully we might get the impression that guilt is only a crippling influence. If we could get rid of all guilt we would be free.

That is not what those psychologists are saying. When they refer to getting rid of guilt, they are referring to unwarranted guilt, the kind of guilt we feel that paralyzes us but has no true basis in moral behavior.

We all need a certain amount of guilt. When we have been unkind or downright cruel, we *should* feel guilt. When we are tempted to do something against our moral code, the feeling of guilt should arise in us. Indeed, the persons most to be pitied are those who are incapable of feeling guilt. One of the aspects of certain criminals that people find most reprehensible is that they are able to perform the most horrendous acts without betraying the slightest feeling of remorse. We see them as cold and unfeeling; other people's lives mean nothing to them.

Guilt means an internalization of the moral code we have been taught. As small children, our parents and other adults told us what was right and what was wrong. They may have slapped our fingers if we did what we were told not to do. They may have forcibly removed us from the situation. If we persisted, for example, in striking our brother or sister, we may have been taken away and put in our little chair in the corner.

Notice what is happening here. Mother and Father tell us it is wrong to hit another child. We do it anyway. We are then taken away and put away from the group. We are being told that our behavior is unacceptable and we are rejected.

But after a little while, our parents will forgive us. We will promise not to hit again and they will hug and kiss us and take us back into their good graces.

If we again start hitting, we will again be rejected. After a while, the lesson sinks in. This behavior is not appropriate and if we want to be loved by our parents we must avoid it. We stop hitting.

At another time our parents are not around and we may again start hitting. This time no one sees us. But in our little consciences the first stirrings of guilt are felt. This is so true that if Mother and Dad arrive unexpectedly, we will stop immediately, before they can say a word.

Thus are developed conscience and guilt.

Now none of this is bad. This is how we learn to control

our own behavior so that we can live in a civilized society. Without such inner controls we would each need a guard to control our ordinary behavior. We would not be able to go down the street or to the store or to our work because we would not be able to trust anyone.

When most members of a society have the same social mores, basically the same ideas of what constitutes appropriate and inappropriate behavior, such early training makes for an ordered and self-disciplined society. Most societies maintain certain principles such as holding that the following are wrong: lying, cheating, stealing, hurting other people either physically or verbally, disrespect or disobedience to elders or persons in authority. Other types of behavior may elicit a wide range of different opinions; these include such things as patriotism, use of obscene language, sexual behavior, business dealings, or political ethics. Here we find, especially in our own country, many different standards of behavior. Unless we have deliberately chosen to reject the teaching of our childhood, we will feel guilty if we act the way others do, if it is different from what we have been taught. In many cases, even when we have chosen a different standard from our childhood, traces of guilt still remain.

In addition to standards of moral behavior, most parents and adults give children the impression that other behaviors which in themselves may be indifferent are inappropriate ways of acting and also guilt-arousing. These may include certain rules of courtesy, order and cleanliness, and household rules. When these are violated, even though the person is an adult and leads an entirely different lifestyle from his parents, he or she may feel a deep sense of guilt. This kind of guilt may be irrational.

Now irrational guilt is the kind of guilt that is paralyzing, because it does not arise from a violation of a moral code. It cannot be removed by forgiveness because truly there is nothing to forgive. It will only be exorcised when the person has destroyed the "tapes" of their past upbringing.

It has often been said that we all carry around in our heads tapes of what we were taught as children. If certain regulations were told us again and again and reinforced by several significant persons in our lives, we are most likely to have very strong tapes. We may have been told by our mother to drink orange juice every day. It would give us the required Vitamin C. This was reinforced so often that if and when we stop drinking orange juice, we will experience a sense of guilt. We are violating a principle that was instilled in us in childhood. Never mind that there are other ways to get our required Vitamin C. Our mother's words stay with us.

Some persons in today's society, with its changing ideas of what constitutes men's and women's roles, find themselves feeling very guilty because they are violating not only what they were told by their parents, but also the example they were given by them.

A young woman who chooses to work full time may find herself constantly feeling guilty. Her mother always maintained that the true role of a woman was to be a wife and mother; anything else was secondary and unimportant. And her mother reinforced her teaching by never working outside the home and apparently being very happy being a housewife. But the young woman likes to work, the family needs the money, and she finds herself rising in a career that means much to her. Although she enjoys her work — perhaps even because she enjoys her work — she finds herself feeling guilty. This was not what her mother taught her she should do.

To counteract the guilt, she may rush home after work and try to do in the few hours remaining of the day all the things that her mother did all day long. She may even take on extra activities such as being part of the PTA or baking for every bake sale at the school. Or she may indulge her children in an attempt to provide them with the "quality" time she wants to give them.

The situation is complicated if her husband adds to her guilt by resenting her work or her satisfaction in it, or the salary if it is higher than his, or the need he has to share the housework. He may be replaying his tapes from childhood in which his father told him that the man was to run the family, that no real man did "woman's work," that he had a right to expect to be served by his wife. Or he may be replaying the tapes from his teenage years when young men are trying to establish their manhood by macho behavior. He feels guilty about his family situation and adds to the guilt of his wife. Even the children sense the guilt of the mother and will add to it too by making it clear to the mother that she wasn't available one time when they needed her, or that other children's mothers do more things with them.

There is enough guilt here to go around for everyone.

What then can we do about the guilt that covers us? Just feeling guilty and asking forgiveness from everyone solves no problems. None of us really likes the person who is always apologizing, especially when no apology is necessary.

Each time we feel guilty, we need to stop and ask why we feel guilty. Is there a real reason for the guilt, or is this something put on us as children or by others which we do not need to accept? As adults we must reach the point where we accept or reject what our parents and others taught us. Most of us will accept most of what we were taught. Our basic moral code will not change. But there are other things we were taught as children that we can reject. Certain ways of behavior are not a matter of a moral code. They are simply customs and as such may change with the times. Our parents may have lived in a different type of community; certainly they lived in a different time of our nation's history; even twenty-five years makes a great difference. And we must remember that they too carried around with them their own baggage of guilt, passed on by their parents. Often these behaviors were never examined, just copied.

The reasons for certain types of conduct are often shrouded in reasons of the past. For every act there is a reason, although the persons behaving in such a way do not necessarily know the reason.

A house guest noticed that his hostess cut off both ends of a ham before she put it in the oven to bake it.

"Why did you do that?" he asked.

She looked at him and thought a while.

"I don't know," she said, "but that is what my mother always did."

Some time later this same visitor met the mother.

"Why do you cut off both ends of the ham when you bake it?" he asked.

She also looked at him and thought.

"My mother did it that way," she said after a while.

This visitor then found himself one day with the grandmother.

"Why," he asked the elderly woman, "do you cut off both ends of the ham when you bake it?"

'Why," the grandmother said, "see, my pan is too small."

This particular example does not involve a moral code, but it is an excellent example of the kinds of behavior we often carry through our lives. We need to examine why we do what we do.

If we feel guilty and there is no real reason why we should, then there is also no reason why we cannot proceed with our new way of doing things. In time we will learn to behave as we choose without feeling guilty. But the patterns of guilt are so strong that, even in these circumstances, we are likely not to behave differently in the presence of our parents, even if we are fifty years old and have lived away from home for more than thirty years.

Besides the tapes from our childhood that continue to make us feel guilty, there are many people around us who continue to try to make us feel bad about ourselves. A salesman at our door may attempt to make us feel guilty if we do not buy his product; indeed, we are made to feel guilty if we refuse to listen to his spiel. Or persons asking for contributions may well play on guilt. They may do this by showing us a picture of a starving child. The implication is that if we do not contribute money, the child will starve. However, we may well ask the question: Who took that picture of the child? Did he just take the picture and allow the child to starve? Now, our concern for other human beings will not allow us to let others starve, but our decision to help with a contribution should be based not on guilt but on our concern for others. We should look at what we can afford to give and make decisions as to whom we will give.

Guilt has a way of taking the joy of giving away from us and, as we well know, the Lord loves a cheerful giver. Similarly, when we travel and see the poor, our wealth and possessions must not be a source of guilt. Rather they should be resources that we understand we are to use to help the world situation. We want to act on the principle of love that Christ came to teach us, not on our concern to alleviate our guilt.

Guilt then is a part of everyone's life. And yet there is a paradox of guilt, as Malcolm France points out in his book *The Paradox of Guilt*:

> Even if the word "guilt" is confined to the socially harmful feelings — the self-recrimination — a guilty person will not normally feel that these are wrong; on the contrary he will often feel them to be both necessary and right. He will also feel justified criticizing other people in order to make them feel guilty. The extraordinary fact is that although people defend themselves with the utmost vigor against guilt, at the same time they cannot really allow themselves to be without it. If they had no other guilt they would accuse themselves of being without conscience and insensitive. Their self-attack is necessary to them, yet they defend themselves with real bitterness when others accuse them of exactly those things of which they are already accusing themselves.

We must then be reconciled to ourselves if we are going to be healed of our guilt. Otherwise, guilt will be crippling rather than liberating. And it is not relieved by acting on it; in fact, it becomes a tyrant. The more one acts on guilt, the more often one feels guilt.

Our guilt needs to be examined and related to what we consider to be our moral code, the adult acceptance of appropriate behavior. When we violate such behavior, we should feel guilty. That is what guilt is for; it is the warning signal within us that what we have done is not acceptable.

This is the kind of behavior for which we can ask forgiveness. We should first ask forgiveness from God, and then from the person we may have hurt. And once we have done that, we need to believe and accept that we are forgiven. Just as we sometimes cannot forgive others, we often cannot let go of our guilt. Although God has promised to forgive the contrite sinner and although other persons in our lives have told us that they have forgiven us, we often still feel guilty. It is something like a security blanket, giving us a warm familiar feeling. We are guilty as charged and we want to be punished. Some people will even punish themselves. They just cannot let go.

Persons who feel guilt themselves also feel rejected by others. In turn they tend to convey a rejecting attitude towards others. A rejecting attitude invites rejection on the part of others and more guilt. The vicious cycle is in operation.

As we work to forgive others and ourselves, we must also learn to let go of guilt. We must launch out into the deep, allowing ourselves the freedom that Christ promised to the Children of God. We must be like the sinful woman who poured out all her ointment on the feet of Jesus. When he looked at her and told her she was forgiven, how do you think she felt? Did she go away fearful, wondering if he really meant it? Did she think that perhaps she should come back again the next day and ask for forgiveness again? Did she allow others who held her in contempt to make her feel guilty all over again?

None of this is very likely. It is more probable that she went away rejoicing in the forgiveness of Jesus. His forgiveness freed her. She would now have the courage to change her life. Let others think what they would. Let others try to instill guilt in her. She knew she was forgiven and she joyfully went about living a new life.

11.

Anger

It is necessary to talk about anger for two reasons. When we are hurt or frustrated, we feel angry and our anger often stands in our way of forgiveness.

The other reason is that there is nothing that makes us feel more guilty and more in need of forgiveness than anger.

Many people have trouble coping with their anger. This may be particularly true of women since they have been taught that women do not display anger; those who do are labeled witches or unfeminine. Some have internalized this teaching for so long that they will not even admit that they feel anger.

Yet anger is a legitimate emotion, just as legitimate as fear, or joy, or sorrow, or happiness. As a natural human phenomenon it is good, as are all of our natural God-given gifts. Yet anger, as it is often handled, brings out the worst in us. We would sometimes simply rather pretend that we do not own this emotion.

The outbursts that accompany the expression of anger are indeed sometimes frightening. People shout at each other, they sometimes say horrendous things. At other times they do worse than shout; they may strike or hurt each other physically. It is no wonder that people often feel very guilty over anger. It is also no wonder that it takes a special skill to know how to handle anger.

Anger is not only a psychological emotion, but it also has physical manifestations. Some people turn a deep red or even purple with rage. Others turn deathly white. Still others do not change color at all. They may just sit quietly, but their body language itself expresses anger. They may cross their arms or stiffen their bodies. Some people shout or raise their voices several decibels when they are angry. Others speak very softly but each word is bitten off with bitterness. Some show it especially in their eyes which may blaze with indignation. Others may simply walk away, but their walk is eloquent. We are rarely in doubt that another person is angry. Interestingly enough, even when others are aware of our anger, we may deny it to them and to ourselves.

It has been said that to express anger is far better than to keep it inside where it works to poison one's system. This is only partially true. Anger may be expressed, but often it is expressed in a way that causes much hurt to other persons. When we shout at others or lash out at them or even walk away from them, we are hurting them. We may even be rejecting them. This kind of display of anger cannot be good for us any more than keeping it inside. The guilt that arises and the harm that needs to be made up may give us tasks for years to come.

On the other hand keeping it inside, even denying its existence, hurts the individual. One may deny anger because he or more likely she has been taught from childhood that violent displays of anger are wrong, even sinful. One does not say, "I am angry!"; one says, "I am disappointed," or "I am annoyed," which is often an amazing understatement. Such sentiments are easier to handle but they solve nothing. If someone "disappoints" me and I say or do nothing about it exteriorly, but nourish the problem within, I may be playing the martyr role. This is not healthy. It makes my life one of secret sorrow which robs me of the joy I need to give zest to my life and the ability to handle the daily ups and downs without getting bowled over. And unfortunately, keeping anger inside is often only temporary. After a while so much anger accumulates that it comes bursting out. That is why a so-called mild person may sometimes manifest a very angry response, totally out of proportion to a situation. It was not the situation, of course, that caused the anger. It was simply the proverbial last straw, the occasion that proved just too much to keep inside.

At other times, one does not erupt now and then like a volcano. Instead, it is possible to see anger in a person who never shouts or rants and raves. This person manifests anger by the way he or she walks and talks or by the way daily work is done.

Anger will come out, one way or another. And if it is not handled well it will hurt oneself and others. Anger cannot be denied. It must be dealt with.

In order to deal with anger, we must start by acknowledging that we all have anger. We have all had enough frustrations and disappointments in our lives to accumulate anger. When we were children, we were often denied things we wanted. Our parents said "No" and as we were children, we had to abide by our parents' decisions. Since then we have had many more frustrations in life, sometimes deliberately caused by others and, at other times, by nothing other than the circumstances of life. We have all been angry and we all have a right to be angry.

After acknowledging that anger is a part of our make-up, let us acknowledge that it is a legitimate emotion. It is useless to say that we should not feel angry over any given occasion. If we feel angry, we feel angry.

Then we learn to deal with it. We all know how we feel when we are angry. It is certainly a source of energy. Our pace quickens. We move faster and we may talk faster. It takes much effort to slow down. We are told to stop and count to ten or maybe one hundred. This slows us down and gives us time to think or to decide whether or not we really want to utter the retort that rises to our lips. But the increase of energy that is generated through anger can be used constructively. We may first need to take ourselves away from the situation in order to use the energy constructively rather than destructively. Some find that cleaning the house or their room is a good way to use that excess energy. Some find that working in the garden, pulling weeds, digging or hoeing, help to drain off the energy and produce a beautiful garden. Some find that simply taking a brisk walk or going to the gym for a workout helps.

Others try to channel their energy into ways that will improve things in our society. Many organizations established to combat social problems were begun by persons who were angry at something that had happened to them. Rather than lash out at society or at certain persons, they put their energy into combatting the problems. Examples of these groups include MADD as well as the organization to locate lost children or runaways.

But often the deep anger has not yet been resolved. If we are angry with members of our families we cannot run away nor can we spend all our time cleaning when we are angry. Nor can we start an organization to combat family problems. We will need to tackle the source of the problem more directly.

It is in these cases that the most skill is required. We must face the issue openly and honestly. A list of questions such as these may help.

1. What is the problem? Here it is important to avoid such answers as these: "My wife is always nagging," or "My mother makes me so angry." These are not the problems. What kind of nagging is a problem to you? Why does your mother make you angry?

It is important to remember that no one else can actually make you angry. Anger arises within us. It is not put on us by someone else. It is quite possible that something one's mother does is always the occasion when we respond in anger. The further question must be raised. Why?

2. Why does this make me angry? What is the cause of this? Does your wife's reminding you of things you must do make you feel like a child? Does your wife remind you of your mother? Do you think your wife believes that if left alone, you won't do what is required? Or is it that

you have a basic disagreement on the way things around the house should be done? Or even a deeper disagreement of values?

When your mother talks to you, do you feel she is not allowing you to be an adult? Do you feel angry because you perceive that she disapproves of your behavior? Do you feel guilty when she criticizes you?

3. What can be done about this? Would it help to talk to your wife or your mother about the problem? Can you do this without allowing yourself to be upset?

This is the most crucial part of the whole procedure. Very often a person will try to clear the air only to find that the result is simply more and deeper anger. But if the problem is really one that needs to be handled, one must handle it in one way or another. One may choose, for the sake of peace, to say nothing and to acquiesce in what the other wishes, but if one chooses this route, he or she should be well aware of what they are choosing. They are allowing themselves to endure something that they often find unendurable. It may later cause even greater problems.

When these difficult discussions are held, it is extremely important to make them as straightforward as possible and to avoid all accusations. One may say something like, "When you remind me every day to wear my sweater when it is chilly, I feel resentful. I feel like I'm a child again," rather than "You always make me feel like a child." We need to give I-statements, not you-statements.

Very often when one decides to initiate such a discussion, one prepares well in advance and even rehearses what must be said. But one must be prepared for an angry response. The other person has not had time to prepare a response and he or she may be quickly on the defensive. Here is the danger point. If one responds something like this, "I do that because you will not wear your sweater and you will get a cold. You need to be reminded."

The danger is that one will say angrily, "See, there you go again, putting me down. I am not a child!"

And the anger rises for both persons.

Far better to respond: "That may be true, but I guess maybe I need to catch a few colds before I remember for myself. My problem is just that I don't like to be told."

Again, one is using an I-statement. My problem . . . not your problem.

These discussions are never easy and often they are not the final word. Human beings are such that they tend to get used to certain ways of behaving and they quickly find themselves repeating their usual patterns of behavior. But if there is a modicum of good will on the part of the persons involved, progress will be made. Chances are that after an intensive and painful confrontation as has been described, both persons will think about what has been said. Anger may still be there, but it will be easier to handle because there has been an open and honest exchange of feelings about the problem.

We can also look here at the issue of forgiveness. We will not only tell the person honestly what the problem is to us, but we will extend to him or her our love and forgiveness. It is probably not the time to say, "I forgive you." At this time, this sounds too much like an accusation (You have done something wrong that needs forgiveness), but it is the time to extend the love and concern that show our forgiveness. And we must make it clear that we are not willing to let this problem come between us.

When we are planning to talk to the person (usually someone who means something to us) about the problem that makes us angry, nothing is more important than to talk the situation over with God first. As we reflect on the problem that comes between us, we need to be able to separate the problem from the person. We love and care about that person too. We want to become closer to that person and we know that as long as the problem remains we will not be able to do so. The situation that arouses our anger must be resolved.

As we pray for help to overcome the problem and to approach the person with love and concern, we will also ask God's forgiveness for whatever we have done to make the problem worse. We all know that almost no problem is entirely one-sided. For every nagging wife, there probably is an irresponsible husband. For every woman who feels that her mother is too demanding, there is probably a mother who feels that she is useless and rejected. When we sink our minds and hearts into the will of God, ask his help in what we do, and pray for forgiveness, we will receive insights into the best way of approaching the person with love. And love truly is the answer. Whenever we talk to someone about something that is painful and difficult, especially at this time, it is most important that we do so with love.

Anger, as we have seen, can be a great source of energy. It can also provide the opportunity for us to grow. Since our anger indicates that something is wrong, some need of ours is not being met, some wound of ours is aching, it can be the great educator. We can use it to look into ourselves and find what needs to be fixed. We ask God's forgiveness for what we have done to make the matter worse. We ask forgiveness if we have offended others. If they ask forgiveness of us, we readily give it. We try to fix what needs to be fixed.

And, in time, the loving peace of God will take the place of the bitter anger we may feel.

12.

Healing

When Jesus walked on earth he spent much time healing people. People who were sick, paralyzed, blind, suffering from all manner of illnesses came to him and asked to be cured. He cured them, one at a time, looking at each one, speaking to each one, often asking them if they really wanted to be cured. Sometimes people came asking for cures for someone else; for example, the centurion for his servant and the Canaanite woman for her daughter. He cured these too because of the faith of the petitioners.

But very often Jesus looked into the souls of the sick and saw a greater sickness. While curing their bodies, he cured their souls too. This happened in Matthew 9:2: "Some people brought him a paralyzed man, lying on a bed. Jesus saw how much faith they had, and said to the paralyzed man, 'Courage, my son! Your sins are forgiven.' "

This aroused a storm of criticism in the minds of the Pharisees. Who did Jesus think he was — God?

"Jesus knew what they were thinking and said: 'Why are you thinking such evil things? Is it easier to say, "Your sins are forgiven," or to say, "Get up and walk?" ' " (Matthew 9:4-5).

And to prove his power, he told the man to get up, take his bed, and go home!

He made it clear that both powers belong to him.

The Sacrament of the Sick was instituted as a healing sacrament, not just to prepare one for a happy death. James speaks of this:

"If one of you is ill, he should send for the elders of the church, and they must anoint him with oil in the name of the Lord and pray over him. The prayer of faith will save the sick man and the Lord will raise him up again; and if he has committed any sins, he will be forgiven. So confess your sins to one another, and pray for one another, and this will cure you" (James 5:14-17).

Today in the Church there is a renewed interest in physical healing. Some persons, working particularly through the charismatic movement, seem to have a ministry of healing. People are again experiencing the wonders of God's healing love through the laying on of hands.

Although the idea of physical healing has never been lost in the Church through the centuries, it has sometimes been overlooked. People pray at the time of physical illness, but they often pray after all doctors and medicines have failed.

Now certainly God often works through doctors and medications and it would be foolish not to seek and accept the help we can get from them. But we need to take healing seriously and we also need to see the connection between physical and spiritual healing.

In the Scriptures Jesus often seemed to claim that sins were the cause of physical sufferings.

For example, Jesus cured a man at the pool of Bethesda, a man who had been sick for thirty-eight years.

"Look, you are well now," Jesus told him. "Quit your sins, or something worse may happen to you."

This doesn't mean, of course, that God punishes sin by making people sick. Rather, spiritual and mental ailments are often the cause of suffering and illness or at least they intensify it. This has long since been recognized by doctors. When we are angry or upset, our blood pressure may rise to unhealthy heights. Some persons have been known to actually give themselves heart attacks just through their anger. Other illnesses, such as ulcers, are caused by stress, and stress is often a result of unresolved conflict in our lives. Asthma, colitis, and many other illnesses may be traced to the lack of peace and harmony in our lives. Dennis and Matthew Linn in their valuable book *Healing Life's Hurts* discuss the evidence that even cancer may be triggered by emotionally stressful situations. This is not to say that persons suffering from these illnesses are not really suffering or that it is all in their minds, or even that they are to blame. These illnesses are truly physical and the person cannot just decide that he will ignore them.

Stress is very much a part of human life today and it is the cause of much havoc. Many people do not know how to relax. Even when they decide to take a weekend off and go to the beach, they spend days planning every detail, worrying about everything from the drive to the beach to what they will do when they get there. They have not learned to let go.

Healing often means letting go, freeing ourselves from those elements in our lives that keep us tied to old habits of behavior, or destructive tendencies, or even the poisons of hostility.

Most of us need a spiritual healing. All the wounds and hurts that we bear, all the guilt, sorrow and regret, all the accumulated anger and hostility, all need healing. So many people are wounded and hurting. So many people fail to forgive. So many people feel unforgiven. So many people are bleeding and wounded all around us.

As we ask forgiveness of God and as we extend it to others, we also need to pray for a healing. We need to pray that God will help us get free of the bonds caused by unresolved conflict and inner hostility.

Barbara Schlemon, who is involved in the healing ministry, states that the greatest barrier people put between themselves and God's healing is lack of forgiveness. She says, "There is nothing that will impede our ability to pray for ourselves or for others more than the unwillingness to forgive. It acts as an invisible barrier between us and the Father which prohibits his blessings from being showered upon us or the ones for whom we pray."

But since true forgiveness is often so difficult, we may need to ask for it and extend it many times before it truly takes hold, even seventy times seven times. She adds,

"It is important to remember that forgiveness is a decision, an act of our will which can be effective when we do not feel particularly loving toward another person. Once we decide to take the step and make an act of forgiveness in prayer, the spiritual mechanism is set in motion for our entire being to respond with love."

"Let go and let God," reads a popular poster.

We need to let go of some of the things in our lives that hold us back. We need to allow God to have some space in our lives to do his work, particularly his work of healing.

III.
Problems of Forgiveness

13.

Forgiving and Forgetting

People have been known to say, "I forgive, but I cannot forget."

None of us lives totally in the present. The past is always with us in some way. It does not remain in the past nor does it stay the same; the present is always colored by the past. We must deal with the past one way or another and we need to do this consciously. Good times in our past are consciously remembered and are the source of joy or encouragement for the present. The conflicts of the past influence us in any of a number of ways. How we deal with the memory of them is what counts. We can punish persons who have hurt us. We can suppress or repress the memories. We can pretend the past never happened. We can consciously choose not to remember the bad times. We can distort the memories to make them easier to live with.

To forgive and forget does not mean that what happened never happened. It means simply that we have chosen to forgive and chosen not to allow the past to color our relationship with the person who offended us.

Forgetting what has caused us much pain is, of course,

very difficult, but we do not deliberately need to dwell on it. Often when one says that he forgives but does not forget, it means simply that he does not forgive.

Of course this is problematic. Pain is pain. But even pain goes away after a while. Illnesses are cured. Wounds are healed. Time helps a great deal. Without an effort on our part, though, the pain will not go away easily. And often we do not really want it to go away.

Letting People Off Too Easily?

One of the problems people have with forgiveness is that they feel that they are letting others off too easily. Someone has hurt us deeply. He or she asks our forgiveness. We know that we should forgive; Jesus so instructed us. But it seems too easy. There is something in us that makes us want them to suffer or feel some of the pain that they have caused us. We cannot quite let go. Still, there is no other way around it; letting go is what forgiveness really is. And it is in the letting go that we are truly freed.

This problem of forgiveness is spoken of by Jean Lambert in *The Human Action of Forgiving* in which she discusses the "forgiveness from above" that some see as contempt for those who have actually been hurt. She is referring to such incidents as when Nazi officers asked forgiveness of God for their atrocities. "God forgives them," she says, "but does that make it right for those who have been hurt?" James H. Cone in *A Black Theology of Liberation* wonders if God takes no sides in the struggle for liberation and easily forgives whites (or others) who have for centuries oppressed blacks. It seems that this is all too easy.

What a strange understanding of God and human beings these concepts are. No one is outside of God's forgiveness. And no one can forgive or be forgiven without the working of God's grace. The same grace that forgives the crimes of the Nazis will work to allow those who have been hurt to forgive. But one element must never be forgotten: Without the grace of God, such forgiveness is simply impossible.

Taking on the Burdens

What is happening when we forgive another human person is in a profound way a sharing of Christ's redemptive mission. Jesus came to take upon himself the sins of the world. With those sins upon his back as his cross he carried them to Calvary and made expiation for them in our stead. His death freed us from our sins and our guilt.

When we willingly and wholeheartedly forgive others we indicate that we are willing to take their sins upon us. Tim LaHaye writes about this problem in his book *Anger is a Choice*:

> "Have you ever wondered why forgiveness is so difficult? It is basically because —
> "The person who is hurt (the offended party) does the forgiving and not the person being forgiven (the offender)."

David Augsburger in *The Freedom of Forgiveness* speaks to the same issue. He says:

"The man who forgives pays a tremendous price
— the price of the evil he forgives!

"If the state pardons a criminal, society bears the burden of the criminal's deed.

"If I break a priceless heirloom that you treasure and you forgive me, you bear the loss and I go free.

"Suppose I ruin your reputation? To forgive me, you must freely accept the consequences of my sin and let me go free!

"In forgiveness you bear your own anger and wrath at the sin of another, voluntarily accepting responsibility for the hurt he has inflicted on you."

No wonder forgiveness is so difficult; it is very costly. It is also one of the human actions that make us most like Christ.

Alan Paton in his book *Instrument of Thy Peace* carries this thought further when he writes of a man he knew who left prison after serving his sentence. During his years of incarceration the man had found God and paid more attention to his faith than ever before. As he left, the prison chaplain assured him that all was forgiven, the past was over and done. But when the former convict tried to live again in his old city, the world had not forgotten his crime or forgiven it. His past was very much remembered. The poor man's hope turned to despair; his faith, to doubt. It seemed to him that God had not forgiven him after all.

Paton comments, "It is here that a great duty falls upon us all, to be the bearers of God's forgiveness, to be the instrument of his love, to be active in compassion. This man's return to the world is made tragic because *we were not there*. God moves in his own mysterious ways, but a great deal of time he moves through us. And it is because we are not there that so many do not believe in God's love."

But What I Did Was Right!

Forgiveness sometimes seems black and white when one has offended another. The one who has offended should ask forgiveness and the one offended should give it readily. But what about when both of the persons involved believe they are right? And often with the highest intentions.

Clare of Assisi ran away from her home to follow St. Francis. She was sure she was called by God to do so, but she never could explain that fully to her father. She suffered that she had been the cause of pain and suffering to her parents. She wanted them very much to forgive her for the pain, but she could not renounce the life to which she was called. Murray Bodo, in his book about Clare entitled *Clare, A Light in the Garden*, writes:

> And it was only when Ortolana, her widowed mother, came to live as a nun at San Damiano that Clare knew some peace over the pain she had caused. *Some* peace, because she never knew whether her father had forgiven her before he died. Her questioning of her mother about this was always met with vagueness and evasion, and Clare continued to weep for him. The desire for reconciliation was so deep that she longed for heaven where she would finally be able to tell it all to her wounded father and hear him say he understood.

Working for Peace

But forgiveness must be more than a passive attitude, a mental and verbal releasing of the other
person. Jean Lambert states it well:

> Forgiveness is not chaff but food. It does not mean
> passively lying down under the foot of the oppres-
> sor, nor immorally condoning wrong done to me
> or by me. It means responsibly doing work in hope
> for peace. It means acting in such a way that the
> burdens of the past are not "simply left in the past,"
> and are not childishly transferred to other
> shoulders. Forgiveness means acting to transform
> burdens into possibilities for liberation in the
> future.

It is this final sentence that needs underlining. Instead of thinking of forgiveness mostly as related to past
actions, we need to think of it as building the future. A
new relationship must now be built, one based on a
deeper feeling toward each other because in the
mysterious ways of God's working, we, the forgiver and
the forgiven, have partaken in God's redemptive action.

Forgiveness is never easy and, at times, it can be
most difficult. It may well be something that we will
struggle with all our lives. Yet ultimately forgiveness is at
the very heart of Christianity, one of the greatest lessons
Jesus came to teach us. And whatever the difficulties,
Jesus himself is there to help us.

14.

Examples of Forgiveness

Through the centuries, Christians, starting with Jesus himself, have all been forgiving persons. Forgiveness, like love, is a mark of the Christian. The early martyrs, such as Stephen, readily forgave their enemies. They were followed by millions of Christians who learned the message from their Master. To be a Christian is to forgive and be forgiven.

As persons received the gift of faith and became Christians, they too have followed the message. Christians do not live lives devoid of misunderstandings, sufferings, or pain inflicted by others. Nor are they themselves guiltless. Rather, they learn to forgive and even to love the ones who have offended them.

Millions of Christians have learned this message. Those whom we call saints seem to have learned it the best. When we read the lives of the saints we are continually struck at how difficult most of their lives were and yet what gentle, kind and patient people they remained. They returned evil with good.

Francis of Assisi was mocked and made fun of when he first followed his Lady Poverty. But his gentle behavior, his refusal to retaliate in kind, won people over, so much so that for a time there was almost an epidemic of young people leaving all and following him.

John Bosco overcame tremendous odds to help the homeless boys of Italy. Nobody wanted those riff-raff around, certainly not on their street! According to Boniface Hanley in *Ten Christians*, at times his enemies used violence against him.

> Political and religious foes were not above hiring hoodlums who attempted to mug, stab, and club the articulate Bosco. Once, while John was teaching, a man opened the classroom window and took a pistol shot at the startled professor. The bullet passed through his cassock under the armpit and never touched him. More than once, messages summoned him to a "dying man's" bedside. The patient was bait used to lure him into some dark alley where a welcoming committee would attack him with clubs, pistols, and knives.

And yet John Bosco never deviated from his work, nor did he allow such hostility to sour his spirit. He was always gentle with other people and was known for his cheerful, even joking demeanor.

A cold and angry spirit is simply not a Christian spirit.

Frederic Ozanam, who founded the Society of St. Vincent DePaul, gave excellent examples of forgiveness. During the upheavals in France in 1848 he worked for justice and compassion for the poor. He was also willing to extend compassion to the enemies of the Church. Because of this some of his fellow Catholics accused him, both in print and in speeches, of compromise and even of complicity with those who were anti-Catholic.

Ozanam was deeply wounded by these accusations, but he would not allow such hostility to make him angry or bitter.

"All my life," he said, "I have followed the poetry of love in preference to the poetry of anger. I will not change now."

These persons were considered holy persons and some have been canonized. But there have been others who will never be canonized. Even Louis XVI, the king during the French Revolution who went to the guillotine, remembered Christ's example at his death.

Christopher Hibbert describes his death: "Having arrived at the top of the scaffold Louis walked across it with a firm step, making a sign to the drummers who for a moment stopped tapping while he addressed the crowd in a loud voice. 'I forgive those who are guilty of my death, and I pray God that the blood which you are about to shed may never be required of France.' "

The list of examples of Christ-like forgiveness goes on and continues to the present day.

Pope John Paul II offered an example to the whole world when he went to a prison in Rome and personally forgave Mehmet Ali Agca, the man who had attempted to assassinate him. In June 1989, the press reported that Agca had received a two-year reduction in his life sentence because of what has been called his "irreproachable conduct." This means that he could be released after 24 years. One cannot help but wonder if this "irreproachable conduct" would have been present if the pope had not offered forgiveness.

It is through forgiveness that we are free to be happy. It is through forgiveness that we help others also to be free. It is through forgiveness that God comes closest to us and we to him.

15.

The Forgiveness We All Need

The Church

We, as the Church, need forgiveness for all we have done through the centuries: the persecutions, intolerance, the military might, the oppression. We need forgiveness for what we have done to indigenous cultures — in Mexico, Peru, the Oriental countries and Africa. We need forgiveness for all the times through the centuries when we have failed to mirror the loving Jesus of the Gospels.

We, as the Church, need forgiveness for not speaking out at times for peace, justice, and concern for the poor, and for not being in the forefront of those who reach out to the weakest members of our society.

We need forgiveness for allowing ourselves to get institutionalized and intertwined with the secular governments so that we sometimes forget that we are to show another way of life, a life that is based on spiritual values, not merely material ones.

Our Country

We, as Americans, need forgiveness for discrimination

through the years that has made so many see themselves as second-class citizens who were, indeed, treated as such.

We, as Americans, need forgiveness for not protecting the weak in our country, for honoring the rich and the powerful, for sometimes allowing different levels of justice for the haves and the have-nots.

We need forgiveness for too many crimes of violence in every form in our country.

We need forgiveness for too many drugs in our culture, both legal and illegal, that ruin so many lives and, indeed, so many nations (e.g. Colombia).

We need forgiveness for too many weapons which jeopardize the safety of both our country and the world and which waste both money and resources, using them to destroy rather than to build.

We need forgiveness for too many wars through our short history, wars that have been responsible for the loss of so many lives of our young men and others.

We need forgiveness for too much luxury when people are starving, for too much concern with material items which we well know can never fill the human heart and which may deprive others of their needs.

Ourselves

We, as individuals, need forgiveness for family fights and misunderstandings, for being too quick to criticize and too slow to find the good qualities of others.

We need forgiveness for harboring and nurturing anger and hostility, allowing it at times to poison our relationships with each other.

We need forgiveness for being the cause of suffering for other people at times, rather than a healing presence.

We, as individuals, need forgiveness for sometimes letting ourselves take out our frustrations on those who were totally innocent.

BUT ...

The Church

We, as the Church, need to thank God that through the centuries, in spite of oppression, so many people have stayed with us, the Church, helped to strengthen us in our weaknesses, and forgave us when we were less than we could or should be.

We, as the Church, need to thank God for all those in our midst who did speak out for the weak and the poor in the name of all of us, who forgave the rest of us for our weakness and cowardice.

We, as the Church, need to thank God for all those who by their lives showed the true image that God wishes his Church to have, a Church that does not allow itself to be an arm of the establishment, a Church that shows true spiritual values.

Our Country

We, as Americans, need to thank God for all the Americans who although they may have been treated as second-class citizens went on to contribute to the country and generously forgave those who doubted they could do it.

We, as Americans, need to thank God for all those who

year in and year out worked for the welfare of the have-nots and who still treat the haves as brothers in Christ.

We, as Americans, need to thank God for all those who fight crime, who do not commit crimes, and especially to those who, although they may have been the victims of crime, do not turn bitter or seek revenge.

We, as Americans, need to thank God for all those who care enough about others to help them fight drugs, and those who have a strong enough self-concept not to need drugs or other stimulants to live their lives happily.

We, as Americans, need to thank God for protecting our country, for all the military people who know to use their power only to protect others and never for aggressive purposes.

We need to thank God for showing us the folly of wars and for the grace he has given that we are now friends with many nations who once were our enemies.

We need to thank God for the multitude of good things he has given us, and to thank him for those among us who keep reminding us that these gifts are to be used not only for ourselves.

Ourselves

We, as individuals, need to thank God for our families and for the love and understanding that exists in them that far outweigh the misunderstandings and problems.

We need to thank God for the many times he has driven from our hearts all anger and hostility with his sweet love of forgiveness.

We need to thank God for the healing others have given us and for the many times that others, through their loving words, have forgiven us.

We, as individuals, need to thank God for all the times when he showed us how to handle our anger, not letting it hurt other people.

In all cases, we will see that the good outweighs the bad, that for every time we need forgiveness, there are many more times that we need to thank God. Love is stronger than hate. Goodness will always drive out evil.

"Where sin abounded, grace did the more abound."

16.

Final Thoughts

Some Quotations To Think About and a Prayer

"The fully forgiven man does not rejoice in his own forgiveness but in the divine love to which he owes it; and his past sin persists in his experience no longer as a source of shame but as the occasion of a new wonder in his adoration of the love divine." (William Temple)

"Forgiveness is the sweetest revenge." (Isaac Friedman)

"Forgiveness is God's business." (Heinrich Heine)

"Forgiveness is the highest and most difficult of all moral lessons." (Joseph Jacobs)

"Forgiveness is the giving, and so the receiving of life." (George Macdonald)

"Forgiving love is a possibility only for those who know they are not good, who feel themselves in need of divine mercy." (Reinhold Niebuhr)

"Forgiveness is the most tender part of love." (John Sheffield)

"Forgiveness is the prerogative of noble souls." (Wilhelm Stekel)

"Forgiveness is the fragrance the violet sheds on the heel that has crushed it." (Mark Twain)

"He who is able to love himself is able to love others also; he who has learned to overcome self-contempt has overcome his contempt for others." (Paul Tillich)

"There is no pain so great that time will not soften." (German proverb)

"Forgiveness ought to be like a cancelled note, torn in two and burned up, so that it can never be shown against the man." (Henry Ward Beecher)

"Forgiveness is man's deepest need and highest achievement." (Horace Bushnell)

Lord, make me an instrument of your peace.
Where there is hatred,
  Let me sow love;
Where there is injury,
  Pardon;
Where there is doubt,
  Faith;
Where there is despair,
  Hope;
Where there is darkness,
  Light;
And where there is sadness,
  Joy.

O Divine Master,
Grant that I may not so much seek to be consoled,
As to console;

To be understood,
As to understand;
To be loved,
As to love.
For it is in giving that we receive;
It is pardoning that we are pardoned,
And it is in dying
That we are born to eternal life.

(St. Francis)

Bibliography

AUGSBURGER, David, W. *The Freedom of Forgiveness 70X7*. Chicago: Moody Press, 1970.

BASSETT, Bernard. *Guilty, O Lord*. Garden City, NY: Doubleday, 1975.

BODO, Murray. *Clare, A Light in the Garden*. Cincinnati, OH: St. Anthony Messenger Press, 1979.

BRUSSELL, Eugene M. (ed.). *Dictionary of Quotable Definitions*. Englewood Cliffs: Prentice-Hall, 1970.

FRANCE, Malcolm. *The Paradox of Guilt*. Philadelphia: United Church Press, 1967.

FREEMAN, Lucy and STREAN, Herbert S. *Guilt: Letting Go*. New York: John Wiley & Sons, 1986.

HANLEY, Boniface. *Ten Christians*, Notre Dame, IN: Ave Maria Press, 1979.

HIBBERT, Christopher. *The Days of the French Revolution*. New York: Morrow, 1980.

LAHAYE, Tim & PHILLIPS, Bob. *Anger is a Choice*. Grand Rapids, MI: Zondervan, 1982.

LAMBERT, Jean Christine. *The Human Action of Forgiving*. Lanham, MA: University Press of America, 1985.

LERNER, Harriet Goldhor. *The Dance of Anger*. New York: Harper & Row, 1985.

LINN, Dennis & LINN, Matthew. *Healing Life's Hurts*, New York: Paulist Press, 1978.

MACNUTT, Francis. *Healing*, Notre Dame, IN: Ave Maria Press, 1974.

MARTOS, Joseph. *Doors to the Sacred*. Garden City, NY: Doubleday, 1981.

McMANUA, Jim. *The Healing Power of the Sacraments*. Notre Dame, IN: Ave Maria Press, 1984.

PATON, Alan. *Instrument of Thy Peace*, New York: Ballantine, 1982.

PLYMALE, Steven E. "The Lucan Lord's Prayer," *The Bible Today*. Vol. 27, No. 3, May, 1989, pp. 176-182.

SHLEMON, Barbara Leahy. *Healing Prayer*, Notre Dame, IN: Ave Maria Press, 1976.

TOBIN, Eamon. *The Sacrament of Penance*. Liguori, MO: Liguori Publications, 1983.

WILHELM, Anthony. *Christ Among Us*. New York: Paulist Press, 1981.